THE ART OF DRAWING AND CREATING MANGA ACTION

THE ART OF DRAWING AND CREATING

MANGA

ACTION

PETER GRAY

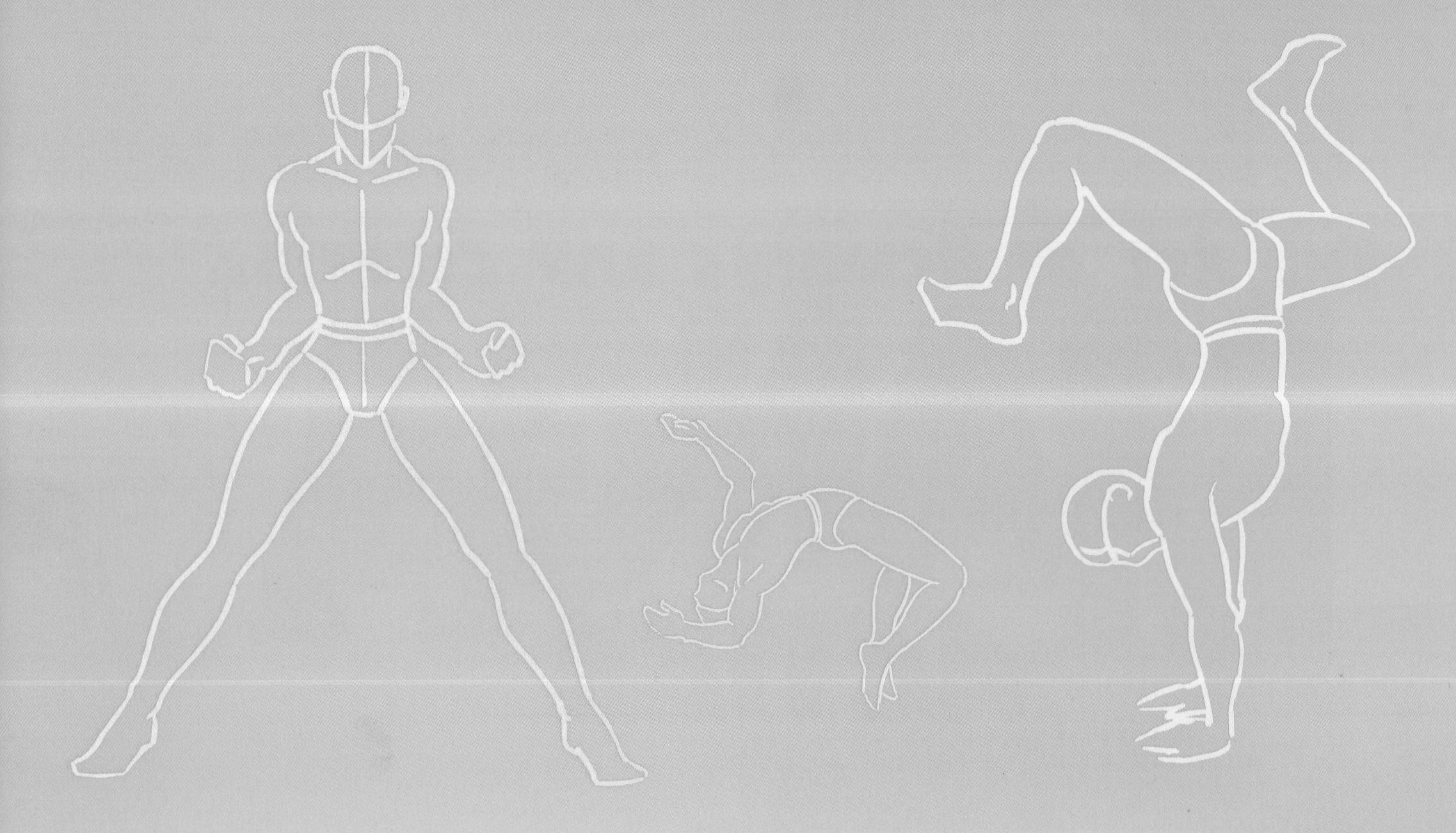

This edition printed in 2005

Selectabook Ltd
Folly Road, Roundway, Devizes,
Wiltshire SN10 2HT

ISBN 1-84193-275-2

Artwork by Peter Gray
Cover and book design by Steve Flight
Digital colouring by David Stevenson

Printed in China

CONTENTS

INTROD

This book is intended to help you understand how to construct the types of action characters that have taken the comic world by storm in recent years and are the stars of Japanese animation (known as anime) like Pokemon, Dragonball Z, Digimon, and Yu-Gi-Oh! Called manga, this style of artwork was first used in Japanese comic books—manga is, in fact, the Japanese word for these original publications.

The style is very distinctive—dazzling eyes, angular features, simple but often exaggerated expressions, extreme gestures, and super-slick coloring.

Every manga character you see in a TV program, movie, comic, or computer game—or on a Web site, trading card, pencil case, or backpack—starts life in exactly the same way, as a rough sketch. The artist then turns this into a black line drawing. Color is added later, and in a variety of ways, as you will discover.

If you follow all the step-by-steps and advice given in this book, you will soon learn all the techniques you'll need to draw manga characters. But drawing manga is more than about just absorbing the theory. To draw well in the manga style takes a lot of practise, so be prepared for some hard work, but a whole lot of fun, too. Once you've built up your skills, you'll be able to create your own original characters, and then there'll be no limit to your sense of achievement or the possibilities ahead.

You never know—one day your creations might make it onto the screen!

DUKE

This is good guy Duke, and he'll be helping to demonstrate some of the drawing lessons in the book. You'll also come across a whole host of other characters from his world—good guys and bad guys.

Duke is 17—he has more muscle than most ordinary teenagers, but he only uses his strength when he has to. He is thoughtful and a bit of a daydreamer.

MATE

RIALS

As long as you can lay hands on a pencil, an eraser, and some plain paper, you can do the exercises in this book. It will help you to use pencils of different hardness at different stages of your drawing.

Pencils are graded from 1 through 3. Number 3 pencils are the hardest—these pencils will make lighter lines. Number 1 pencils are softer and will make darker lines. Most general-purpose pencils found at home or school are graded Number 2. Use a hard pencil, like a number 3, for sketching the guidelines you'll be drawing to help you shape your characters; using this pencil ensures the lines are easily erased later. Use a softer pencil, like a number 2 or number 1 when you're ready to pick out all the final lines of your drawings to darken them. Mechanical pencils are best, as they produce a constant fine line. If you're not using a mechanical type, make sure you keep your pencil sharpened.

You'll also need an eraser—you can use any type, but make sure it doesn't leave dirty marks.

You can use any odd scraps of paper to make your initial sketches—my manga characters often start life on the back of an old envelope or shopping list. Most of the pictures created for this book were drawn on cheap photocopier paper. You only need to think about the quality of the paper you are using if you are coloring your pictures using materials like watercolor paint, which might make the paper tear or buckle.

THE HEAD

In manga-style drawings, female faces tend to be quite similar—even the bad girls are usually pretty and even-featured.

Male faces vary much more because for manga boys and men, the main emphasis is on character and action rather than beauty. Male faces can be fat or thin, long or round, square or heart-shaped, cheerful or sinister, handsome or downright ugly!

In this section, we'll be looking at a whole range of male faces and bodies. We'll start by focusing on Duke's face since drawing his face from a variety of angles will teach you the basic skills you need in order to draw all kinds of other manga characters.

For each drawing, we'll start by sketching some guidelines to form a framework for the head. We'll then add more guidelines for other features step by step. You'll want to erase most of these lines at some point, so don't make them too heavy. Use your hard pencil to draw them or, if you only have a soft pencil, press lightly so the lines are fainter.

My guidelines are dark in this book to make sure you can see them clearly to copy them. In each step, I've also made the new lines red so you know exactly what to do.

THE HEAD
THE HEAD
THE HEAD
THE HEAD
THE HEAD
THE HEAD
THE HEAD
THE HEAD
THE HEAD
THE HEAD
THE HEAD
THE HEAD
THE HEAD
THE HEAD
THE HEAD
THE HEAD
THE HEAD
THE HEAD

Front View

For each step, study the picture carefully to see all the lines that you need to draw.

Step 1

Start by making a basic framework. First draw a vertical line to help you make your picture symmetrical. Draw a circle over it and add four lines to form the sides of the face and jaw. Draw a horizontal line halfway down this whole shape. Add a short pencil stroke for the mouth.

Step 2

Eyes are roughly halfway down the head—Duke's irises are round, and the tops should touch the underside of the horizontal line. To draw the ears, start level with the tops of the eyes. The ears should finish level with where the bottom of the nose will be. Draw outline shapes for Duke's hair, neck, and collar too.

Step 3

Add the pupils, eyelids, and eyebrows, then use two long curved lines to mark the bangs.

Step 4

The main feature to work on here is the hair. Duke has a middle part, so the hair will hang symmetrically. It also has an angular look.

Step 5

A small circle in the top right of each eye makes the bright highlights that characterize manga artwork.

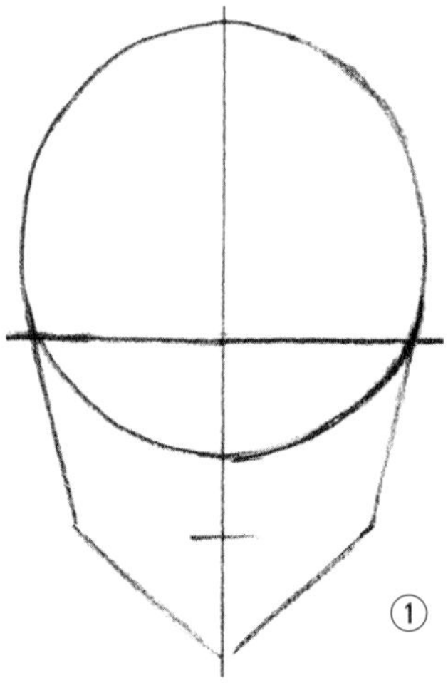

①

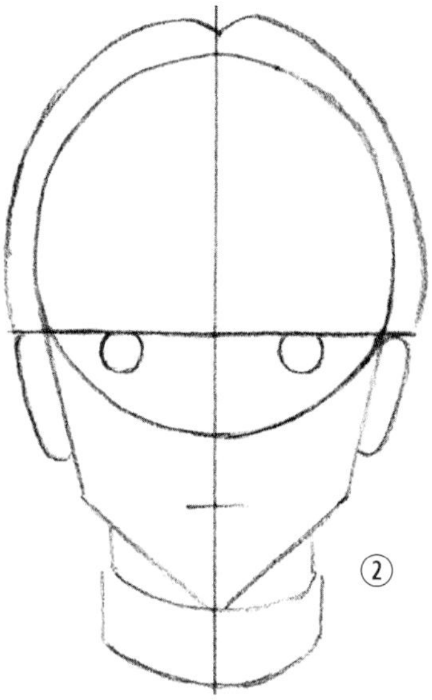

②

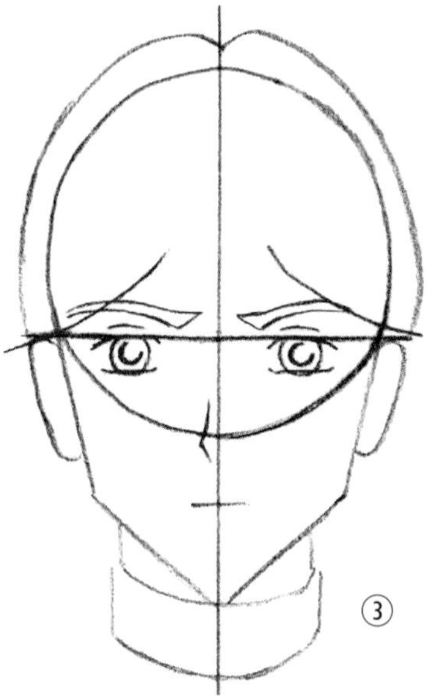

③

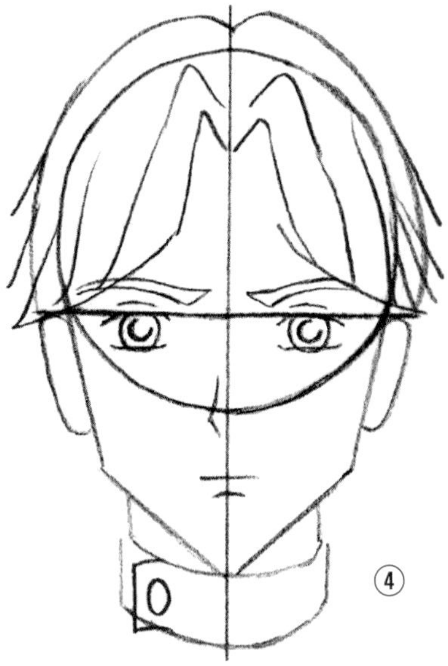

④

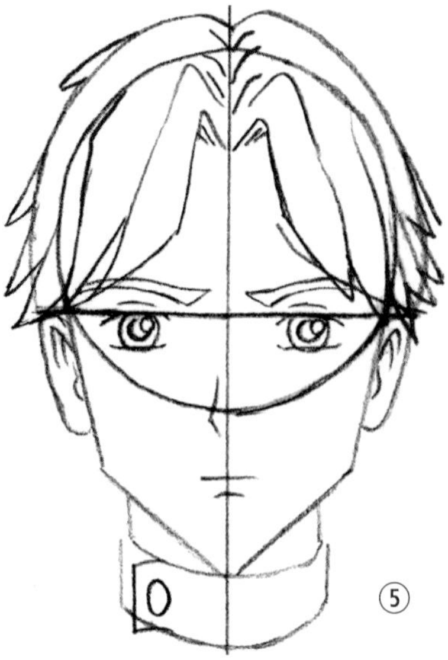

⑤

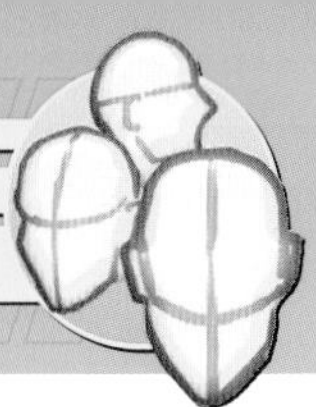

Step 6

Now ink over all your final pencil lines with a black ballpoint or felt-tip pen. Use long, confident pencil strokes for the pieces of hair that hang over Duke's forehead. Shade in Duke's pupils, but leave the bright highlights white. Once the ink is dry, erase the rest of the pencil marks—especially the ones that made up your original framework.

You can copy the colors I've used here or wait until you've worked through the Color section of this book so that you understand more about how to apply color.

6

The eyes of most manga characters are spaced more than a whole eye's distance apart. There's more information on drawing eyes later in this book.

Profile

When seen from the side, Duke's skull is based on an oval-shape.

Step 1

Copy the framework for Duke's head. The vertical guideline drops down from the oval to form the front of the face. The horizontal guideline should sit halfway down the whole head shape again.

Step 2

Place Duke's eye and ear, starting on the horizontal guideline. From this angle, the eye takes the shape of a narrow oval, and sits near the front of the face; the ear is just over halfway back. The neck slopes backward slightly. To outline Duke's hair, roughly follow the shape of the top of the head, then curve your line in toward the back of the neck.

Step 3

You can see here how the vertical guideline helps you shape the front of Duke's face. Work on the eye and add the eyebrow. Draw a long curve to mark the length of the hair.

Step 4

Duke's hair is cropped close to the neck at the back. Copy its shape. A slight curve to the jaw makes for a much more pleasing profile.

Step 5

Add a few more lines to Duke's hair, particularly at the top to show how it hangs down from the parting. From this angle, Duke's pupil and the bright highlight should both be oval-shaped not round.

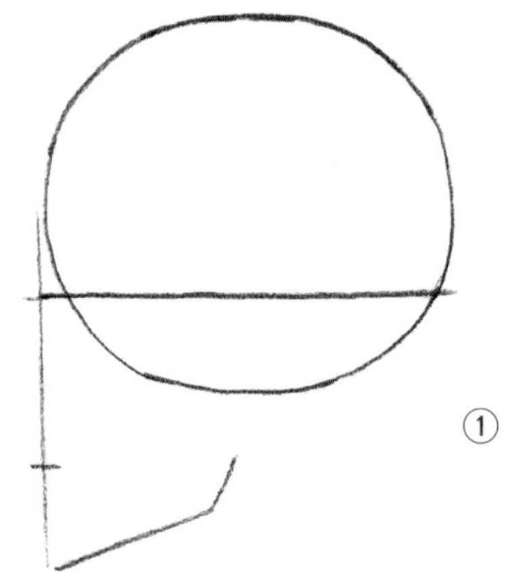

①

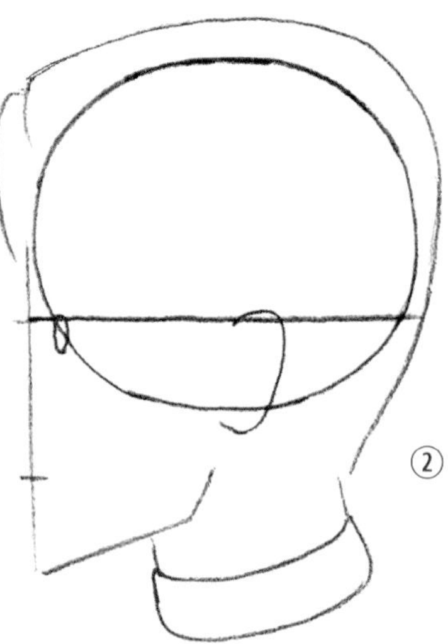

②

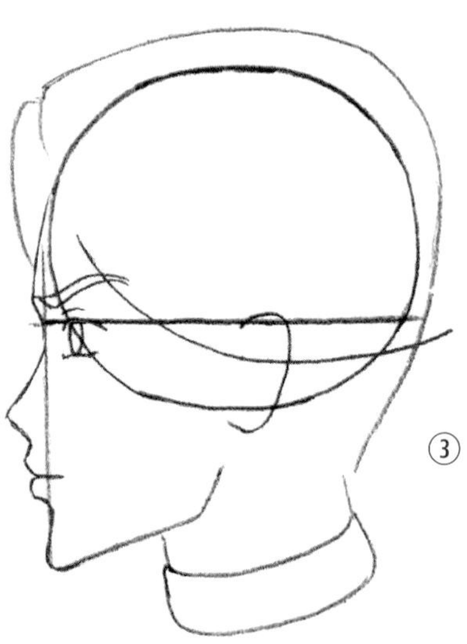

③

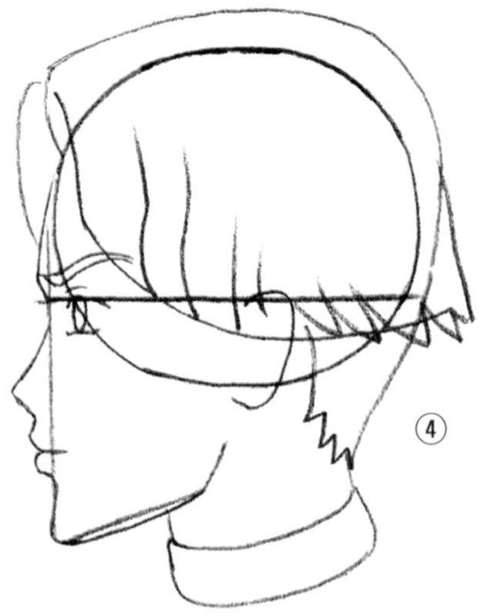

④

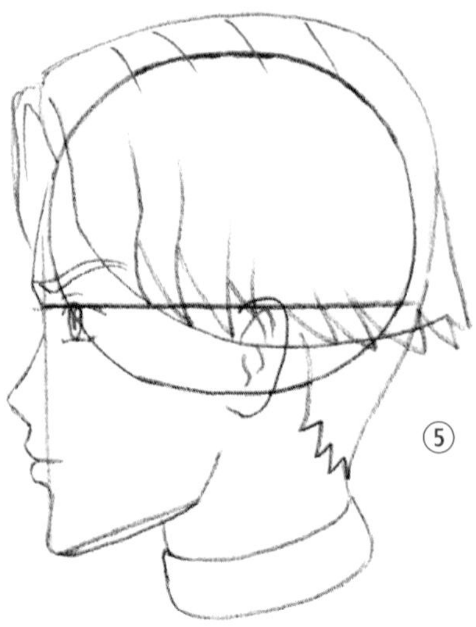

⑤

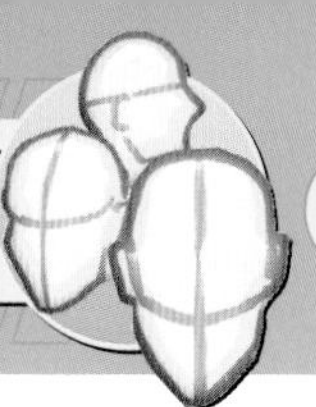

Step 6

When you're happy with your picture, go over your final lines again using a black ballpoint or felt-tip pen. Notice how while I was doing this, I decided to add a couple of tufts to the crown of Duke's hair. I also made the line of his neck more curved at the front. Let the ink dry, then erase the rest of the pencil marks to leave a clean drawing.

⑥

¾ View

Duke has turned his head so that we can see both the front and side. This angle is slightly more complicated to draw, but mastering it is worth the effort.

Step 1

Copy the shapes that make up the framework of the head—start with a circle that's slightly elongated and tilted to the right. The vertical line marking the center of the face has moved in the same direction as the head and curves at the top. The horizontal guideline is still halfway down the whole shape.

Step 2

When you place Duke's eyes, notice that the iris of the one on the right of your picture is almost circular. The one turned farther away is slightly smaller and oval-shaped. It also sits closer to the vertical guideline.

Step 3

Add some detail to Duke's eyes and draw the eyebrows—we can't see all of the eyebrow on the left of the picture. Re-shape the jawline to make it less angular.

Step 4

To draw Duke's nose, start level with the bottom of the eyes. Don't forget the crease line on the chin.

Step 5

The main thing to notice here is that the bright highlight on the eye to the left of your picture is more of an oval shape, just like the iris.

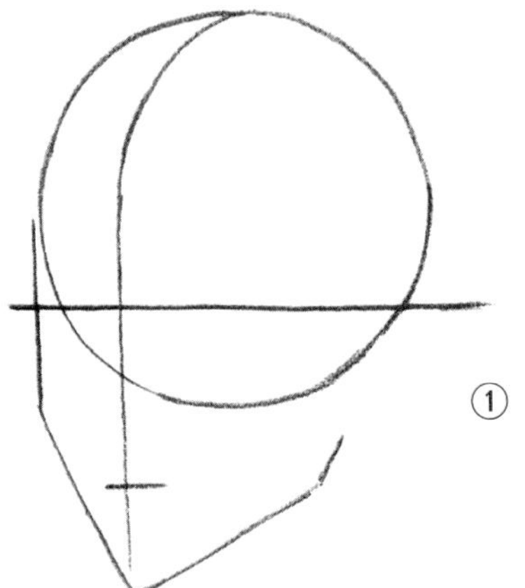

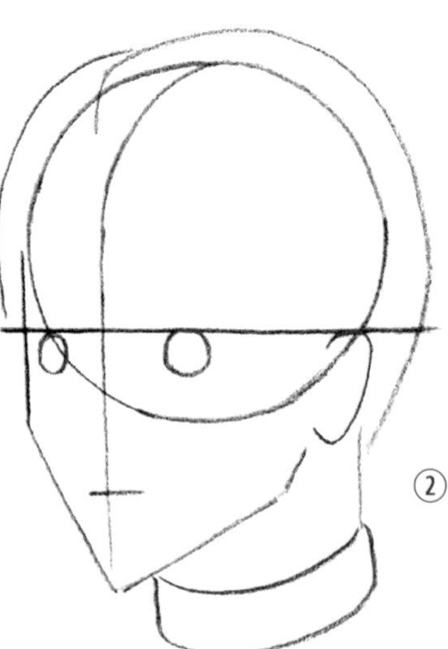

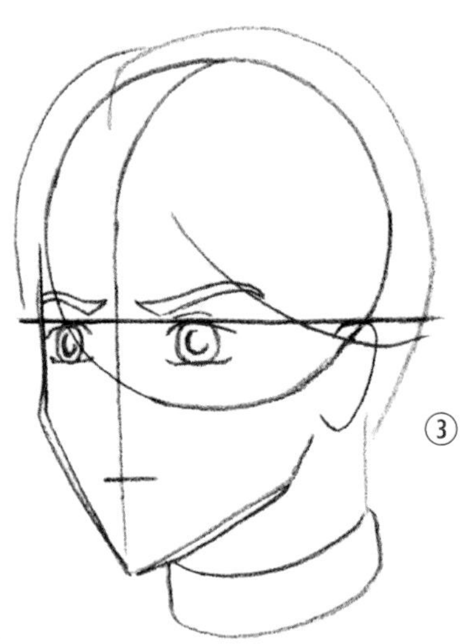

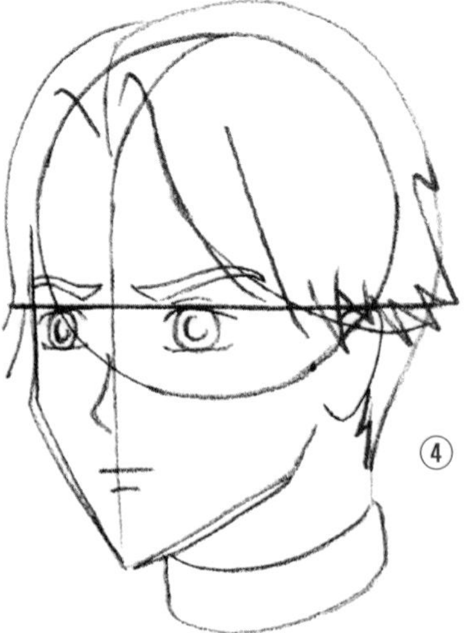

Step 6

Take another look at your picture. If the face seems crooked or squashed, look back over steps 1 to 5 and see if you can work out where it went wrong. If you need to start again, don't worry—remind yourself that practice makes perfect. Once your drawing looks similar to this one, go over your pencil lines with a black pen. Notice how I've added a few extra little lines to the hair and collar here to give them more definition. When the ink is dry, erase the rest of the pencil marks.

⑥

Different Angles

Like real people, manga characters move their heads in lots of different directions, so you need to be able to draw them from all angles. Some angles are trickier than others, but if you always use guidelines, you'll be much more successful at drawing well-proportioned faces. Look carefully at the way the guidelines curve in the next series of pictures.

① When Duke looks down, the top of the skull looks almost circular—its curve forms the guideline that helps you place the eyes and ears. We can see a lot of his hair and all the facial features are low down. The ears sit higher than the eyes.

② If Duke tilts his head up to one side, his hair becomes less prominent and we can see a lot of his face. Now the ears are lower than the eyes. The eye to the left of the picture is closer to the guideline running down the center of the face than the other eye.

③ If Duke is looking down at an angle, we can see a lot of one side of his hair and his face takes up a much smaller proportion of the picture.

④ The farther his head turns the less we can see of Duke's features.

⑤ Seen from this angle, all we get is a close-up of the cut of Duke's hair, his neck and ears. His features aren't visible.

Proportions

The pictures here show Duke at various ages. They demonstrate how the relative proportions of a face change as a person gets older. The horizontal lines will help you to see exactly how the proportions differ.

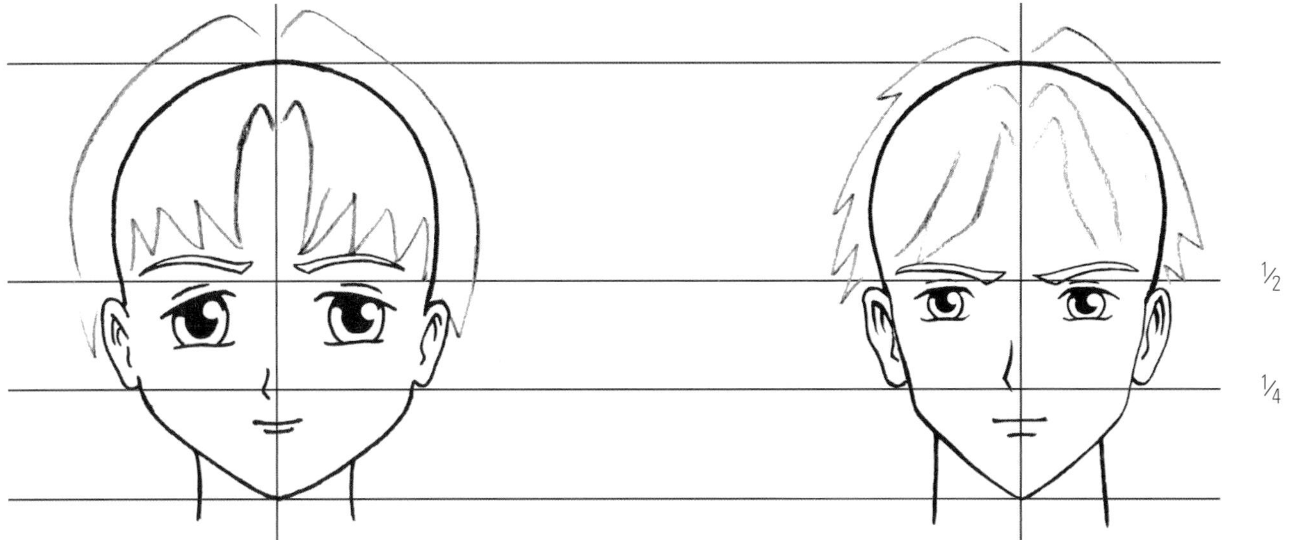

At the age of nine, Duke's eyes were large in relation to his other features and sat below the center of his head.

Duke is 17 at the moment. His eyes appear smaller, and they are higher up on his head than when he was a boy.

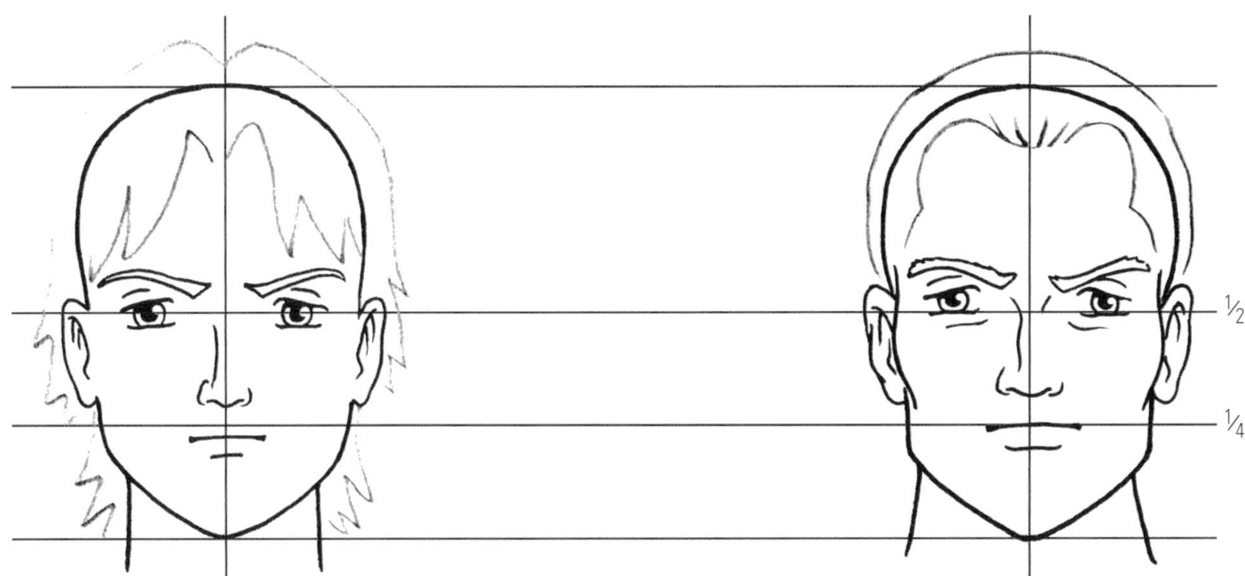

By the time Duke is 25, his eyes will sit halfway up his head. His nose and mouth will have grown much bigger.

As Duke gets older, his eyes sit even higher on his head. The mouth and nose continue to grow.

Expressions

The human face is capable of revealing a very broad range of emotions. Good comic artists are able to show in their drawings different moods and reactions to help with telling a story and building character types.

Here Duke is making some of the facial expressions that are common to male manga action characters. With the aid of a mirror, you can use your own face as a model for any expression you want to capture in your drawings.

Simple changes >>

Creating different expressions may seem complicated, but it's really about making very simple changes. Here are some dramatic expressions you can practice drawing—each one is made up of just a few simple lines and circles.

Perturbed

Angry

Injured

Curious

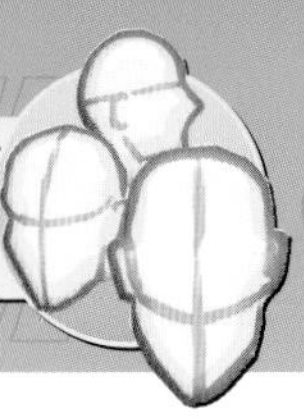

Good Guys & Girls

Inventing characters is one of the most rewarding aspects of drawing. Here are some I've made up. You know they are good guys because they have large pupils, even when they have small irises, and their expressions are soft. You can tell they have different strengths, weaknesses, interests, and attitudes—it all shows in their faces.

Streetwise Teen

Young Scamp

Smouldering Beauty

Tough Guy

Minx

Fantasy Hero

Serious Type

Schoolboy

Dreamer

Try drawing each of these characters or make up some of your own. Try changing the expressions, whilst retaining the friendly features of each face.

Good Boy Jai

This character, Jai, is much younger than Duke—you can tell by the shape of his head and the features on his face. You will draw him in a similar way, but the proportions will be different.

Step 1

Copy the framework for Jai's head as shown. His head isn't as long as Duke's, so make the lines forming the outline of the face and jaw much shorter. The horizontal guideline will still sit halfway down the shape, but since Jai is looking down slightly, the ends of this line will curve upward.

Step 2

Jai's eyes are large in relation to his other facial features. One eye is hidden by his hair, but the one we can see has a large oval-shaped iris.

Step 3

Add the detail to Jai's eye and draw a large eyebrow. His nose is smaller than Duke's, so make it short and rounded. Soften the jawline.

Step 4

Now work on Jai's floppy hairstyle. He has a side part—notice how this affects the way the hair falls.

Step 5

Jai has two bright highlights on his eye—a large almond-shaped one fills the top corner and a second one, shaped like a tiny oval, sits underneath this.

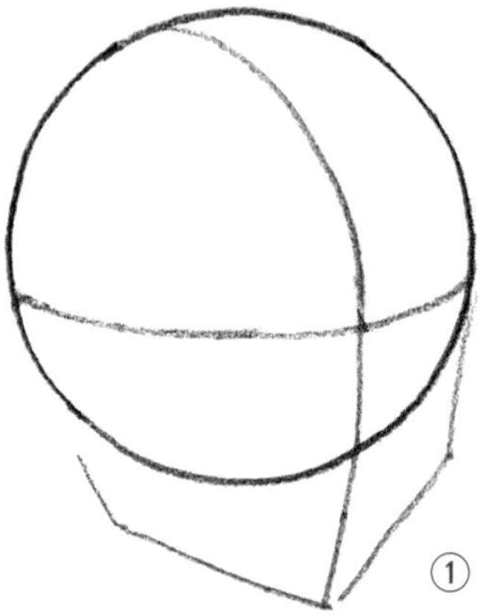

①

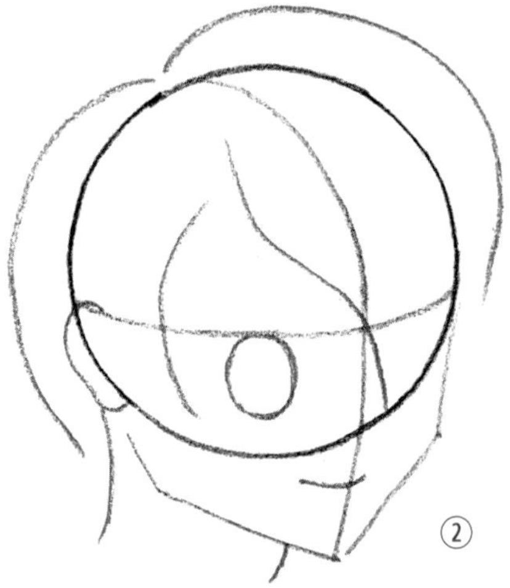

②

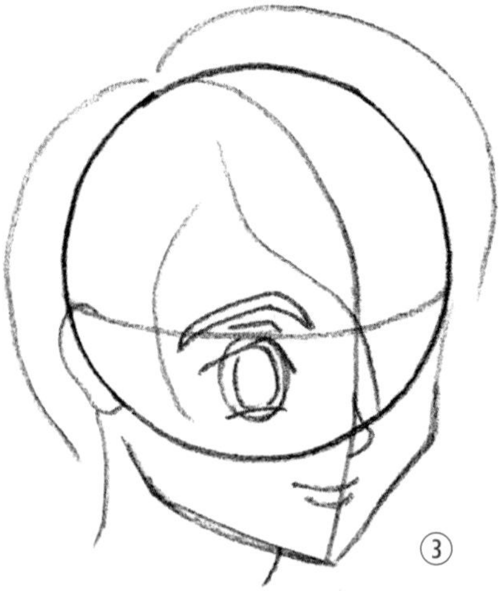

③

④

⑤

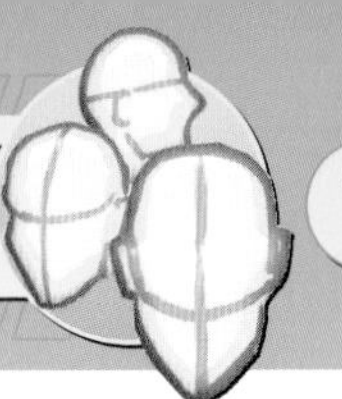

Step 6

Ink over your picture. Give the ear more definition if you think you need to. Shade in Jai's pupil, making sure you leave the bright highlights white. Leave it to dry, then erase any pencil lines that formed the original framework for the head.

If you add color to your picture, try making the smaller bright highlight a light blue instead of white. Make some areas of the hair paler to show the way the light hits the hair.

⑥

Bad Guys & Girls

Most bad guys have tiny pupils and dramatic eyebrows. They are also usually much uglier than bad manga girls! After you've tried drawing the examples on this page, how about inventing some bad characters of your own?

Loco

Aggressive

Cunning

Sly Thug

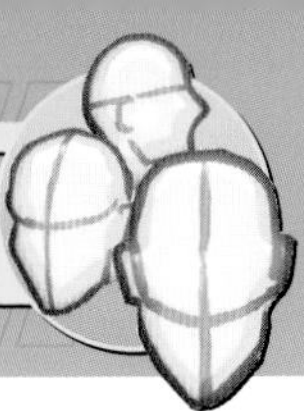

Venomous

Manic

Schemer

Freaky

Spiteful

Eyes

When you are drawing manga eyes, keep in mind that the eyeball is round—it doesn't always look like it because some parts are hidden by the eyelid. Nearly all manga eyes have a white spot on them; a bright highlight to make them look shiny.

①-② Looking straight ahead

The eye has a round iris (the colored part of the eye) and a round pupil (the black spot in the middle). The top part of the iris is shaded black because the eyelid is casting a shadow over it. The bright highlight is left white.

③-④ Turning away

When a head is turned away, we can see more of the white part of the eye. The farther a head turns, the narrower all parts of the eye become. The iris, pupil, and white highlight will all sit farther and farther to the right. To draw a narrow eyeball, start with a circle, then add a curved line to it just in from the left—think of this curve as where the skin covers the eyeball.

⑤ Evil eyes

Changing the shape and details of the eyes can immediately turn a good character into a bad one. Cover up more of the eye with the eyelids and make the iris and pupil smaller.

①

②

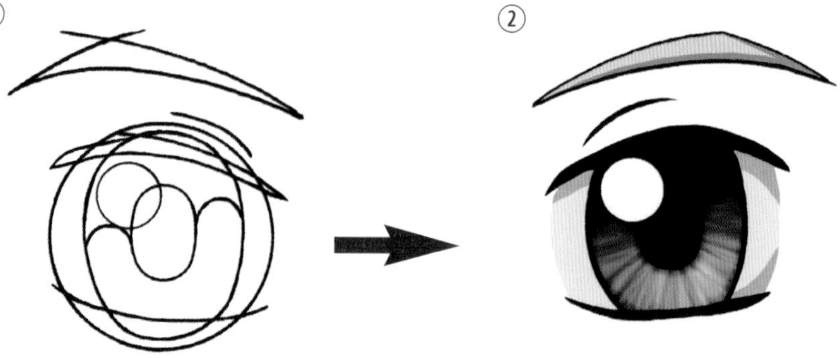

③

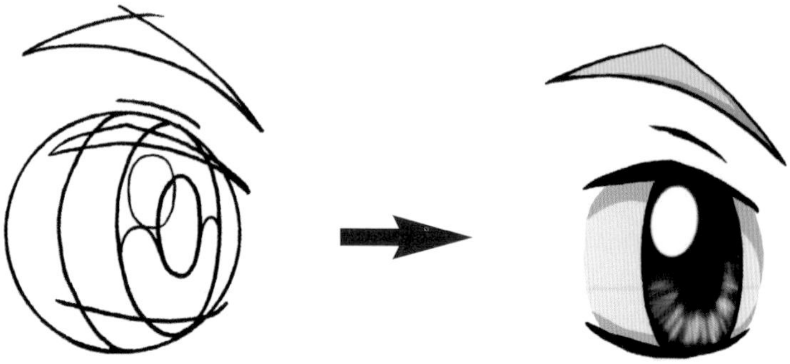

④

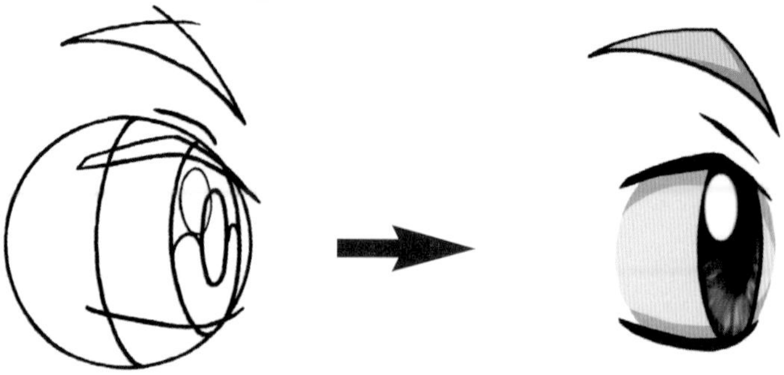

⑤

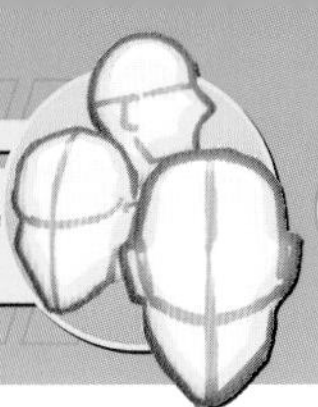

Nasty Duke

Here is Duke's evil twin Dagger. By comparing these pictures of the manga twins, you can see that just a few small alterations to Duke's facial features turn him from a kind and innocent teenager into a mean and aggressive bad guy!

Make the eyes narrower and give them smaller pupils. Angle the eyebrows down toward the center and draw two deep frown lines in between them. Add some little lines at the top of the nose to show that Dagger is sneering. Now change the shape of the mouth so Dagger is curling his bottom lip. Notice how subtle changes to the color and shading adds to the effect too—a dark shadow is now cast across the eyes.

Bad Guy Bile

Getting the framework for Bile's head right is the key to creating this evil character.

Step 1

Start by drawing a circle with a vertical guideline curving down from the top. Carefully study the picture to copy the other vertical guidelines. Add the horizontal guideline—it should curve slightly as shown.

Step 2

Draw two small circles for the irises of Bile's eyes—notice how one sits slightly higher than the other. Copy the curves of the eyebrows. Draw the first lines of the nose, mouth, and ear and add the thick-set neck.

Step 3

When you draw Bile's eyeballs, position them so that the irises sit high up inside them. Copy the crooked shape of Bile's face and jaw. Add two little curves to form the edges of his wide nostrils.

Step 4

The eyebrows really make Bile's face look mean here—make them jagged along the top to show how hairy they are. Don't forget the lines that create bags under his eyes.

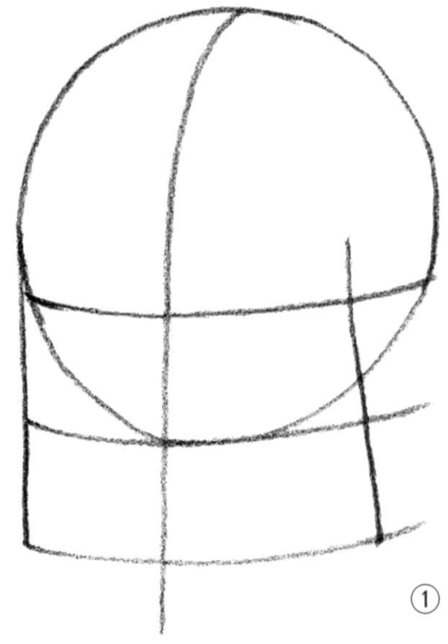

①

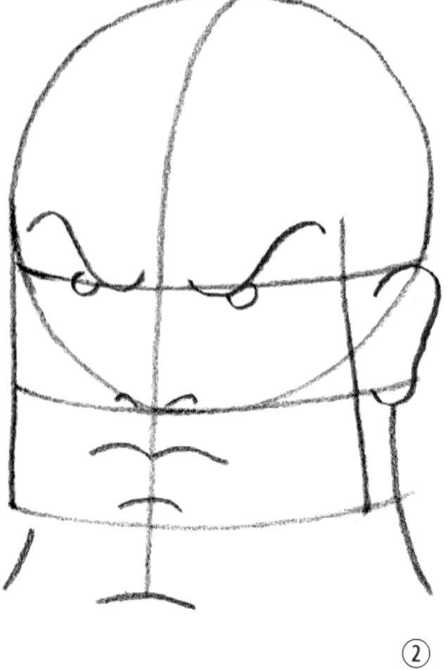

②

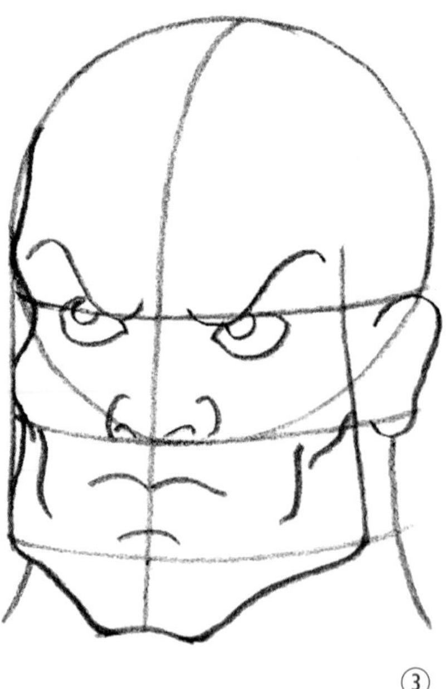

③

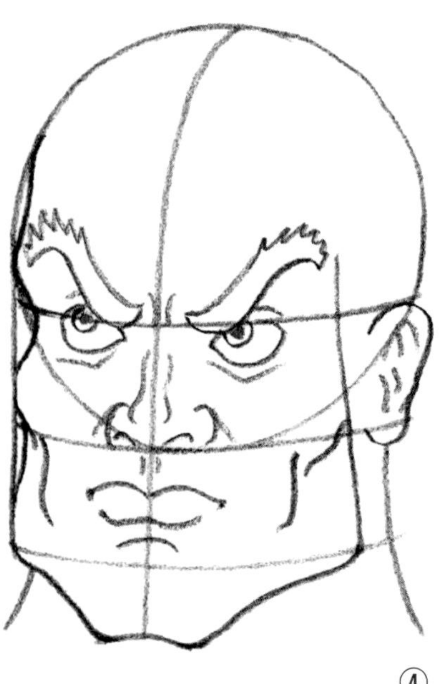

④

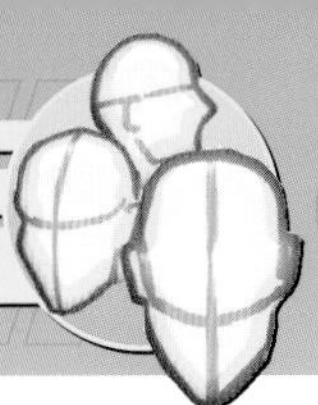

Step 5

Now go over your heavy pencil lines using a black ballpoint or felt-tip pen. Go over some of the lines twice to make them bolder—study the picture closely to see where I've done this. When the ink is dry, erase any remaining pencil lines, including the ones that formed the original framework for the head.

Now you can have some fun with color. I've turned Bile a sickly green and added a tinge of gray around the eyes. The orange eyebrows look like they're on fire.

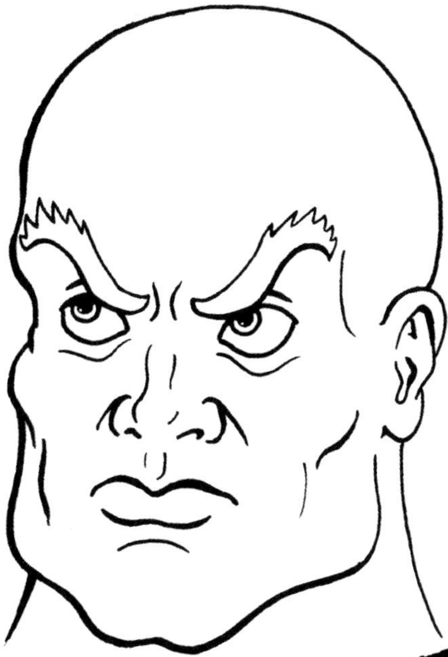

⑤

THE FIGURE

Now that you've had some experience drawing heads, you need to learn how to draw the bodies you'd attach to them to get your character moving.

The human body is a very complex machine with bones, muscles, fat, and skin all working together. You don't need to understand its entire makeup to draw a manga-style figure, but knowing something about the structure of the skeleton, and the flesh and muscle attached to it, will help make your drawings easier to construct, so that the final results are much more effective.

It might take a while to master all the various lines involved in drawing the body from different angles, but you'll start to work it out after a few exercises.

To help you understand how the shape of the body changes as it moves, study your own body in the mirror—stand at different angles and try making a variety of poses.

The Skeleton

The skeleton can be thought of as a frame that you hang muscles, skin, and clothing on. The arms don't hang directly from the chest but are separated by shoulder bones. The legs are joined directly onto the hips. The body is able to bend because of the joints—the arms have shoulder, elbow, and wrist joints whereas the legs have hips, knees, and ankles.

① Simplified front view

This is a simplified version of the front view of Duke's skeleton to show the main body parts. The joints are drawn using dots.

② Simplified side view

When Duke is seen side on, some of his features get thinner and others disappear from view. Notice the arch of the spine from this angle.

③ Simplified ¾ view

As Duke starts to turn toward the side, the shape of his rib cage and hips will look different again.

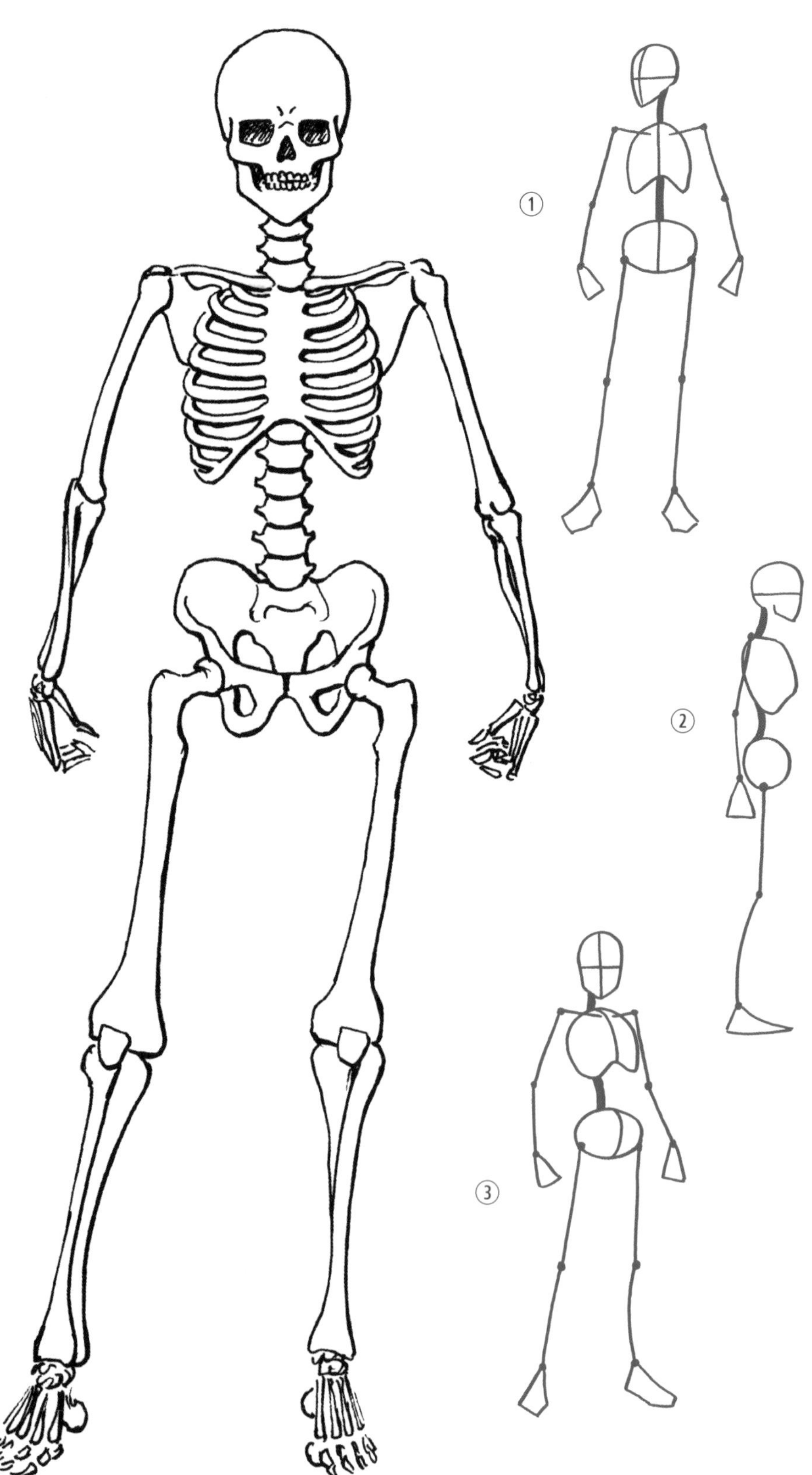

Muscles

Duke is a typical manga teenager—larger than life. A real boy of his age would probably carry far less muscle than this.

① Body outline—front view

Duke's outline mostly follows the shape of the skeleton—it curves out more where the body is particularly muscular, and tapers in at the joints.

② Muscles—front view

③ Muscles—side view

④ Muscles—rear view

These pictures of his body show how the flesh and muscles wrap around Duke's bones. Study these pictures carefully. Understanding the muscle structure under the skin will make drawing it easier. You may like to refer to these pictures when you are drawing your own action characters.

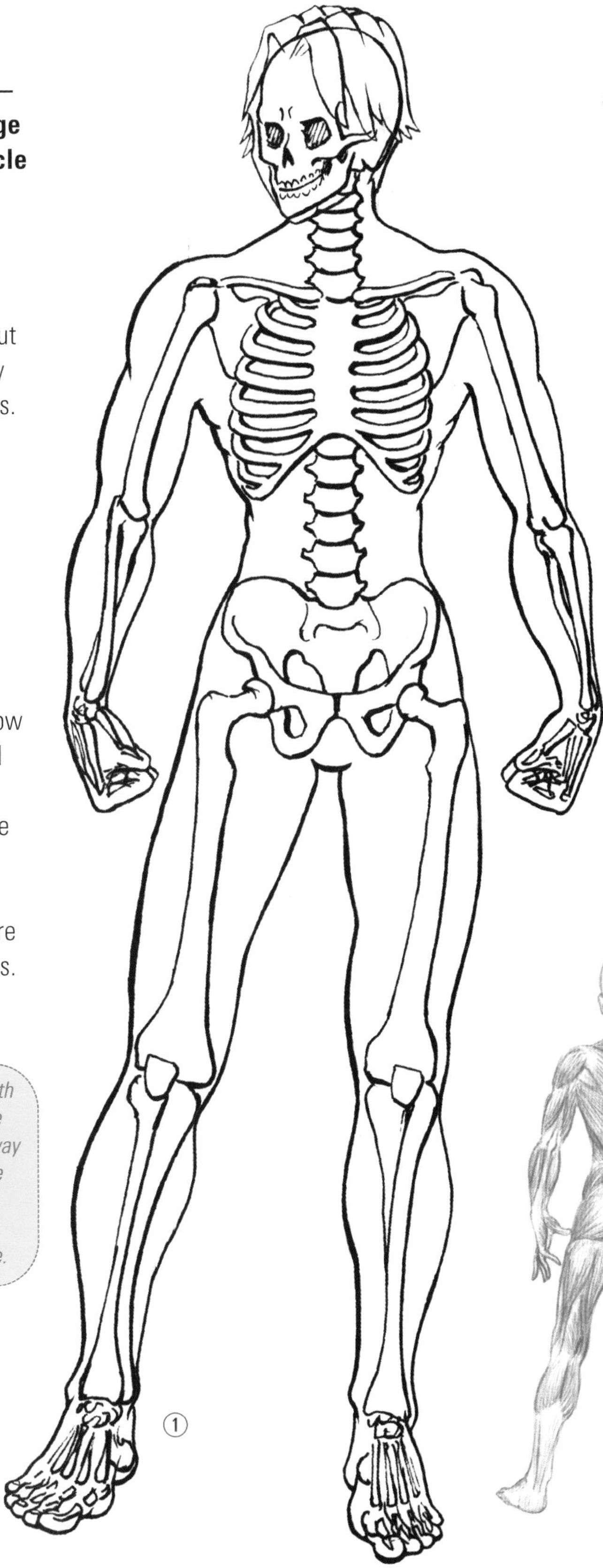

To draw a character with a larger build, draw the body outline farther away from the bones and use stronger curves. For a skinny body, keep your lines closer to the bone.

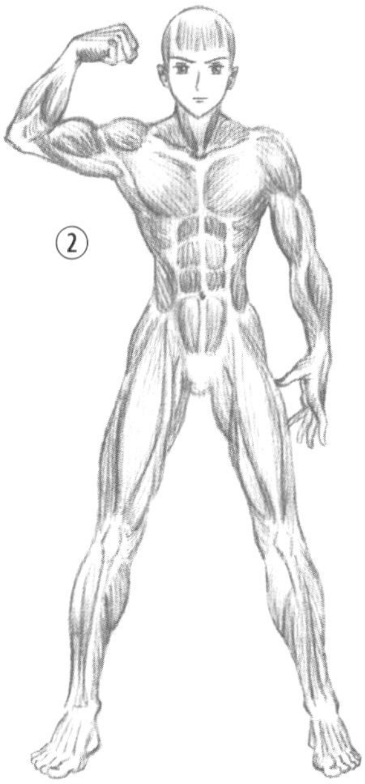

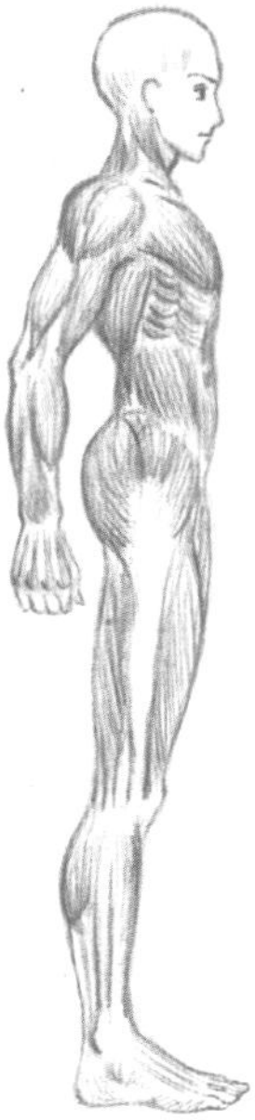

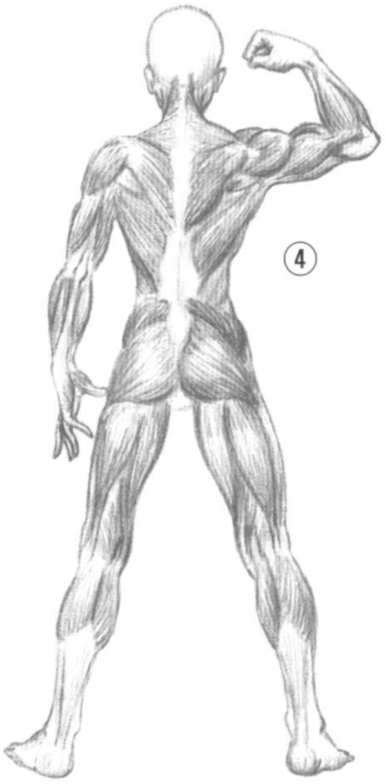

Front View

This is Duke's body as viewed from the front. This is the easiest angle to draw, so it is a good one to start with.

Step 1

Start by drawing a vertical line to help you make your picture symmetrical. Draw the framework for the face as you learned to do on page 12. Copy the shape of the chest here—it's a large oval that curves in at the bottom to represent the shape of the rib cage. Now draw an oval lying on its side to make the hips. The gaps in between these body parts are for the neck and stomach. Add the limbs (arms and legs)—notice how much longer the legs are than the arms. Use dots to mark all the joints. The hands and feet can be drawn as simple triangles to begin with.

Step 2

Add some rough guidelines to mark where the flesh and muscles will go—don't worry about the joints yet. Copy how these lines curve farther away from the bones around the more muscly parts of the body like the shoulders and calves.

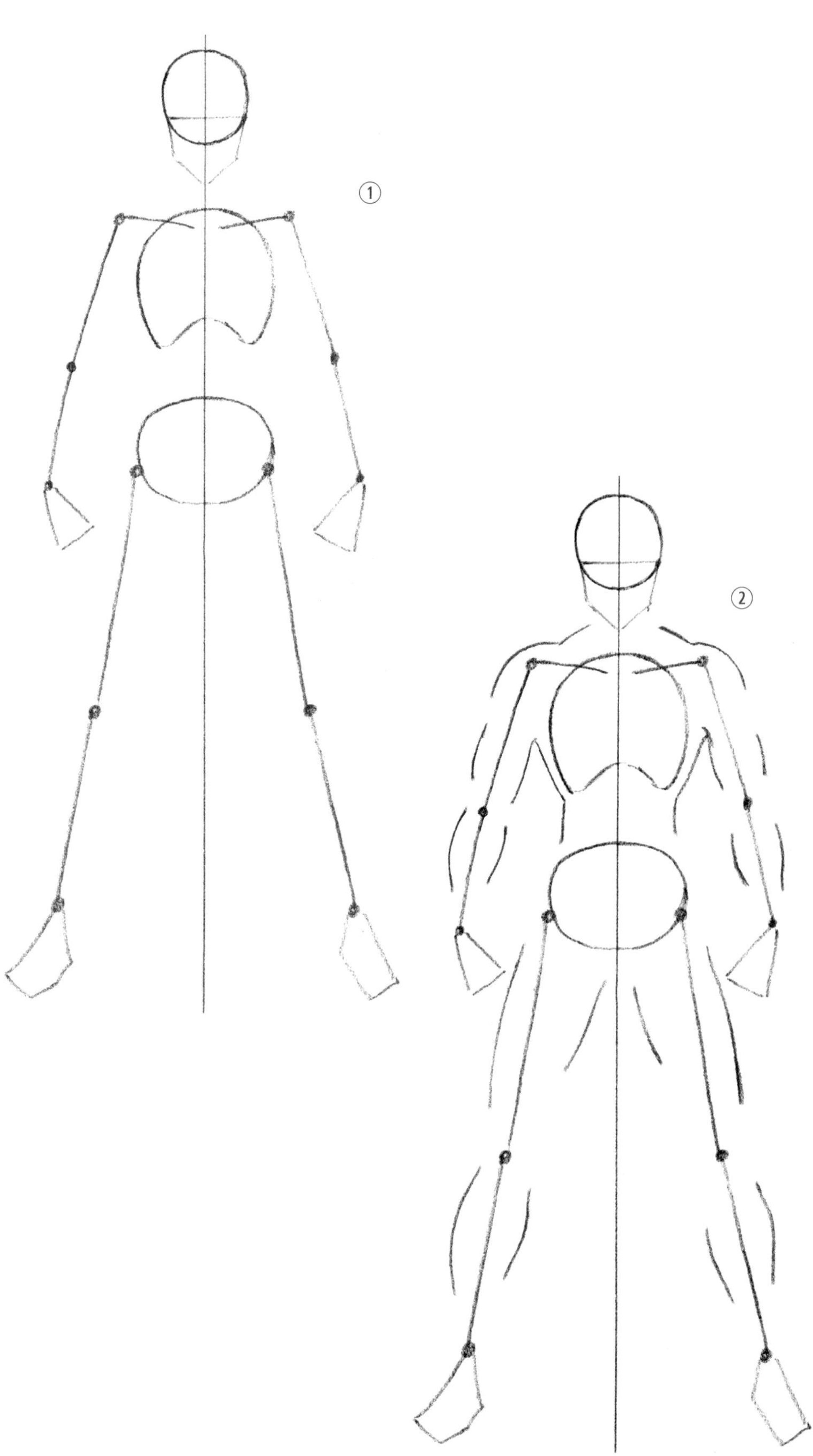

Step 3

Start joining together the parts of the outline you drew in the last step. Carefully copy where the lines curve inward like at the elbows, wrists, and ankles.

Step 4

Now it's time to give the muscles on the upper body more definition by drawing some curved lines on the arms and chest. Copy the pattern of the shapes that form the stomach muscles. Try holding your hands like Duke's and looking at them in the mirror to help you work out how to draw them. We'll look at drawing hands in more detail later in the book. When you finish the outline at the bottom of the legs, copy how it juts out at the ankle bones. Copy the curves of the toes and the ball and heel that you can make out on the inside of each foot. When you've sorted out the main parts of the body, outline the hair and facial features, remembering what you learned in the Head section of this book (refer back to pages 12–13 if you need to refresh your memory).
>>

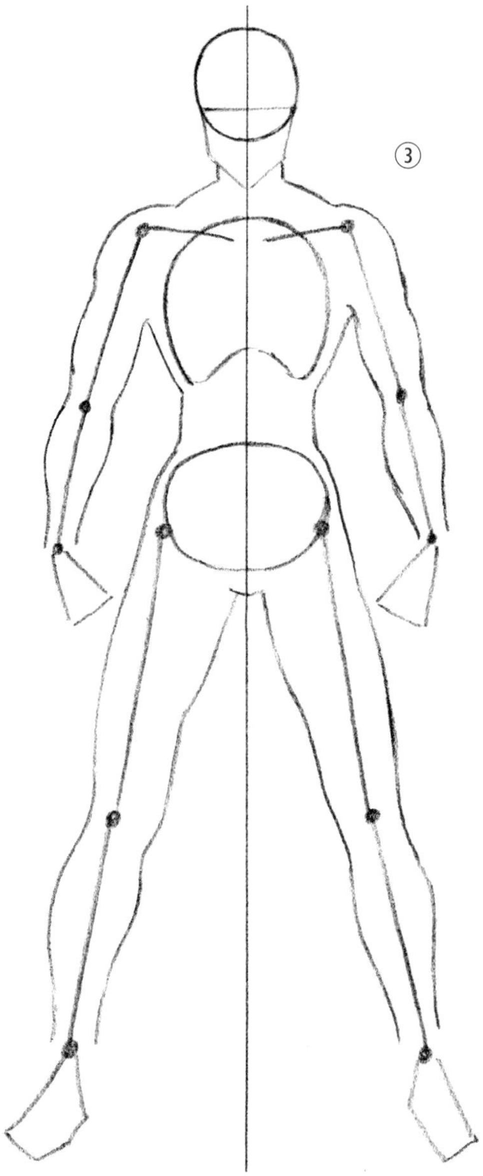

It's important to get the basic shape of the feet right—they won't look realistic if you square off the toes. Practice by drawing your own feet.

③

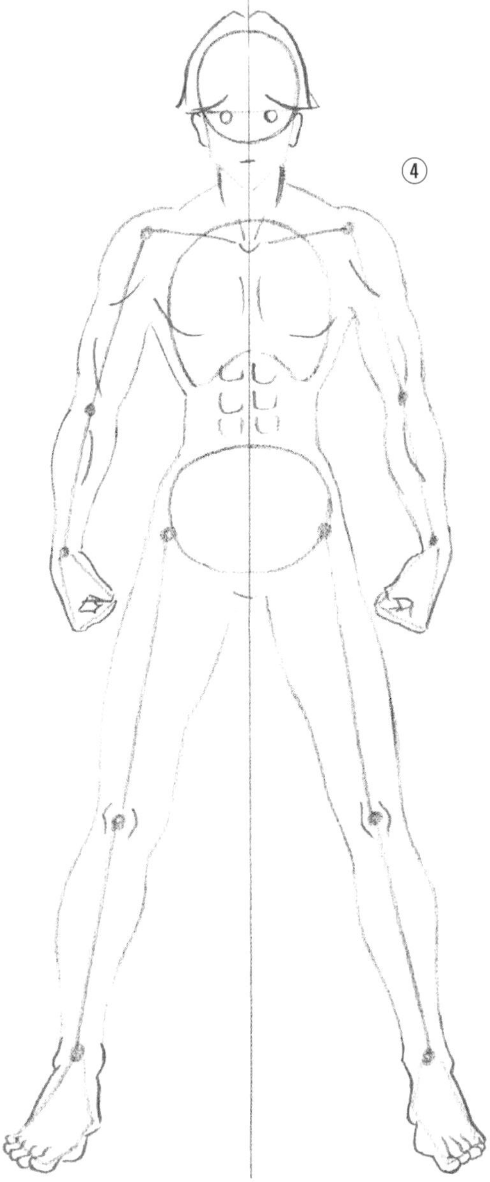

④

<<

Step 5

Go over your final pencil lines with a black felt-tip pen or, if you don't have one, a ballpoint pen. Mark the lines of Duke's swimming trunks and give his fingers and toes more definition as shown. Work on the face and hair too. Add some extra little lines and curves to Duke's body to highlight where his muscles and bones protrude.

Step 6

When the ink is dry, erase all the guidelines you drew for Duke's skeleton. That's your first manga body finished!

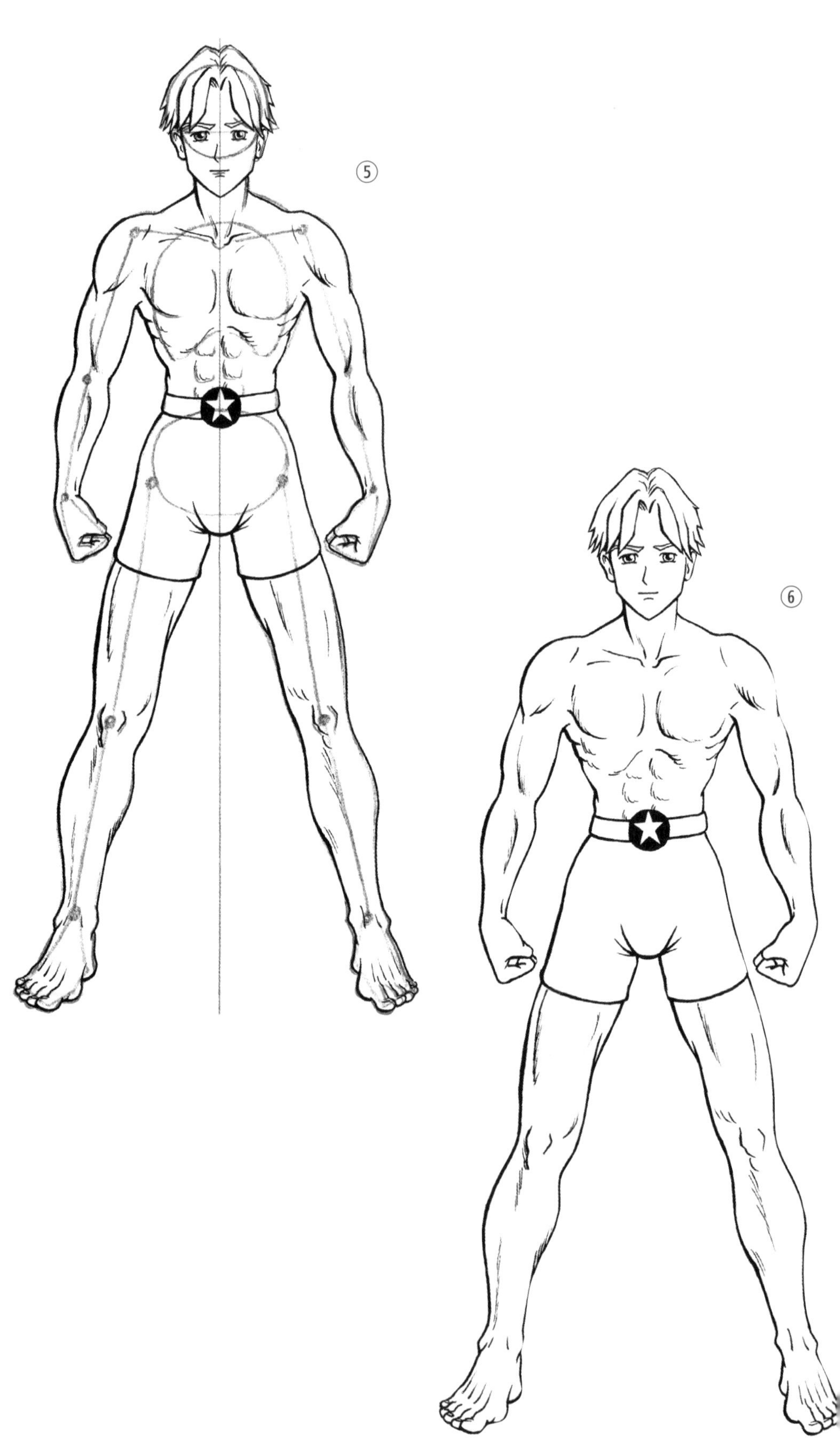

Now you're ready to color in the picture if you want to. Notice how I've shaded some parts darker than others—turn to the Color section of the book for some tips on this.

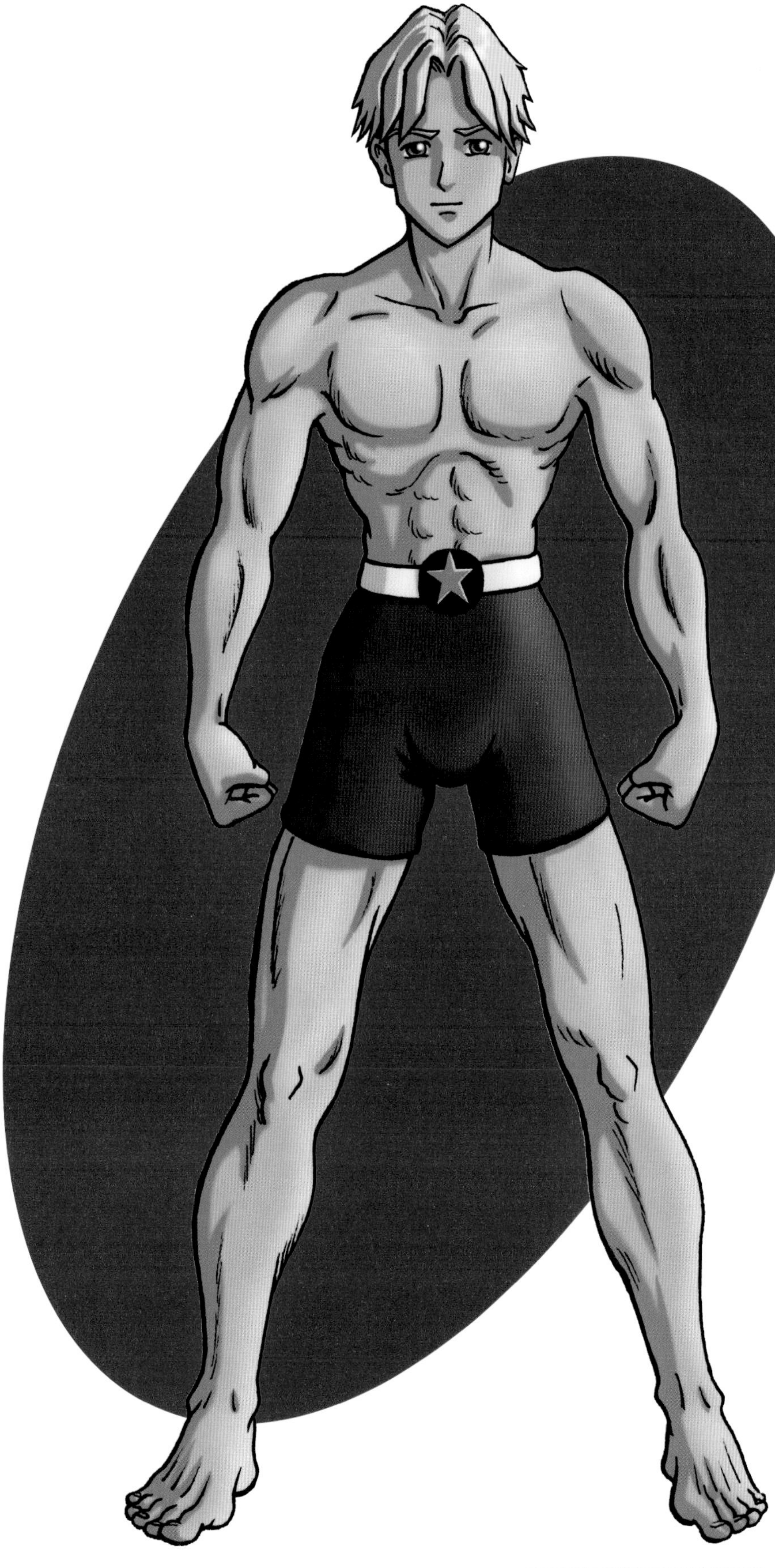

Profile

Duke has turned to the side and changed his pose slightly. When he stands like this, we can see only one arm and one leg.

Step 1

First draw the head, chest and hips. You need to shape the head as you did on page 14 except that Duke is now facing in the opposite direction. The chest is a tilted oval shape with a piece missing near the bottom. The hips are almost circular. Add the curved lines forming the neck and lower part of the spine. Carefully copy the way the limbs are attached to the body. When you draw the leg, curve out the calf bone.

Step 2

Now for some flesh and muscle. Draw some rough lines around the main bones of the body as shown. It's very important that you get these right before you start thinking about completing your outline.

①

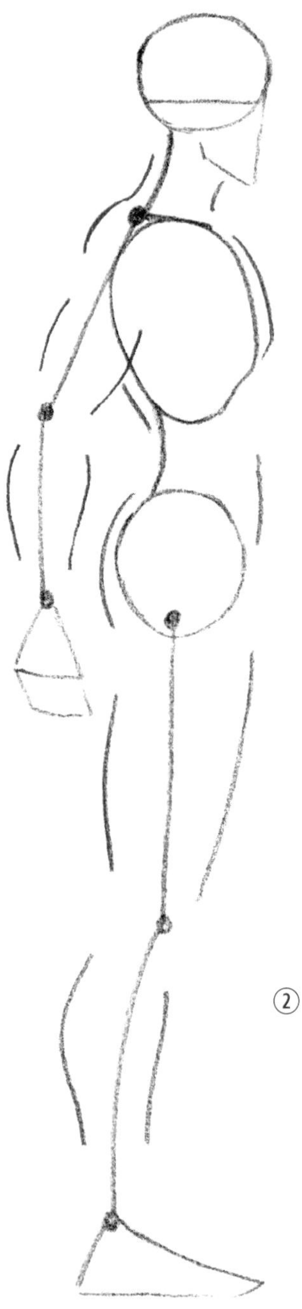

②

Step 3

Once you're happy with where you've placed the main parts of your body outline, fill in the gaps. Study the picture to see how the outline curves in and out around the joints. Notice how the stomach is made up of short curves to define the muscle.

Step 4

Now add some lines to the upper body to make the muscles stand out. You may find it helpful to refer to the muscle diagrams on page 37. Shape the hands and feet, outlining the fingers and toes. Add a little line around the knee and ankle bone to define these. Next start working on the outline of the hair and place the facial features.

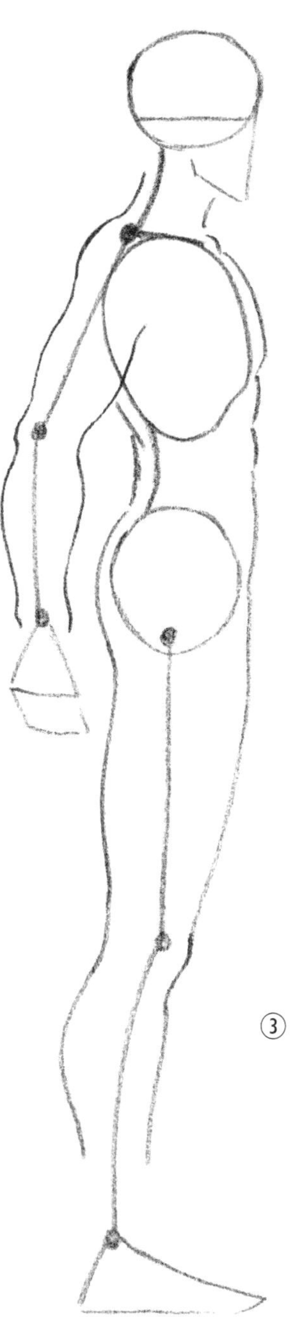

③

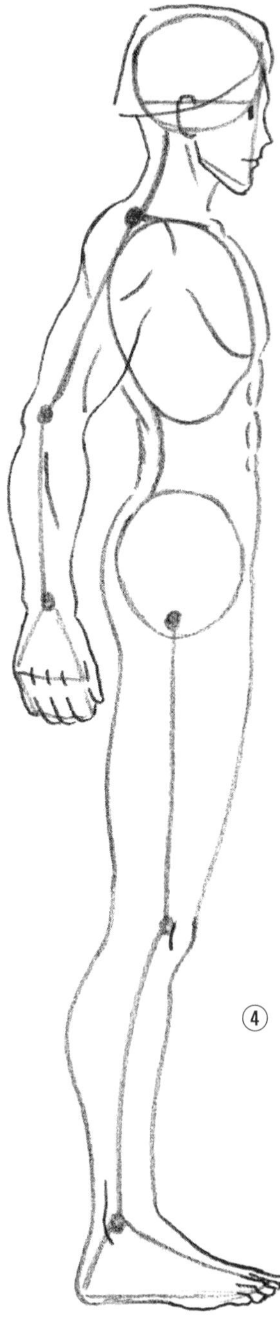

④

<<

Step 5

Draw on Duke's swimming trunks—you won't be able to make out the shape of the star on the waistband from this angle. Now go over your pencil lines with a black felt-tip or ballpoint pen, adding more detail to the hair, face, hands, and feet as you go. Draw some extra little lines around the chest bone to define the rib cage. Study the picture to see where else you could add some lines to emphasize the muscle or bone, like on the neck and thigh. Small details like these can make all the difference to your final picture, making it much more lifelike.

Step 6

Once the ink is dry, erase all the pencil lines of your skeleton framework to leave a clean drawing.

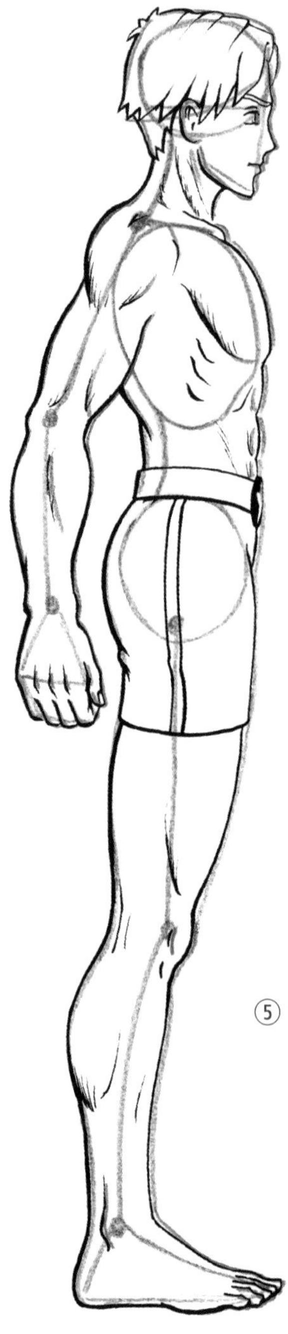

⑤

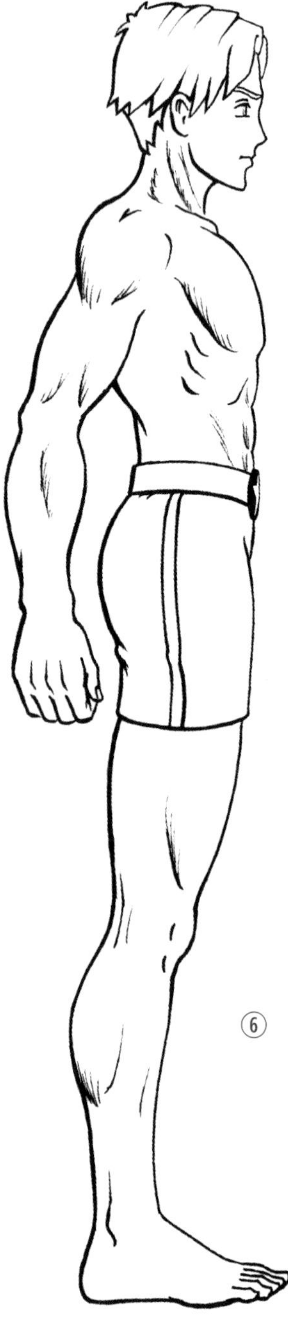

⑥

Now color in your picture if you want to—you could try experimenting with different color schemes to change Duke's hair color and skin tone as well as the design of his swimming trunks.

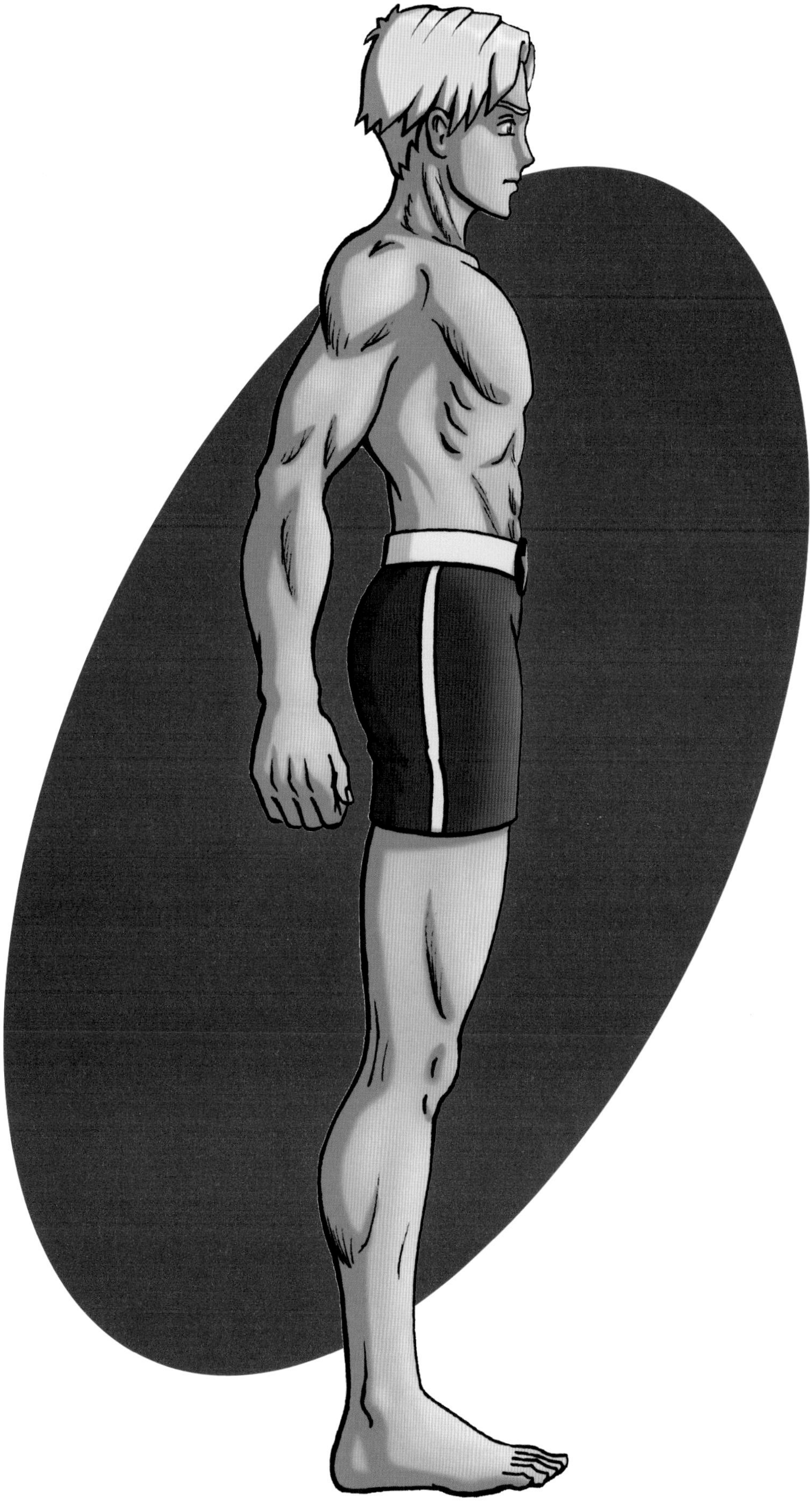

¾ View

This viewpoint is slightly more complicated to draw, but it creates a much more interesting picture, so it's worth spending some time trying to get it right.

Step 1

Remembering to use light pencil lines, draw the skeleton framework as shown. Notice how each of the main body parts has a curved vertical line on it—the lines all curve out to the right. The lines for the neck and lower part of the spine also curve out to the right. Position the limbs as shown.

Step 2

Add the main lines that mark the flesh and muscle around your skeleton framework.

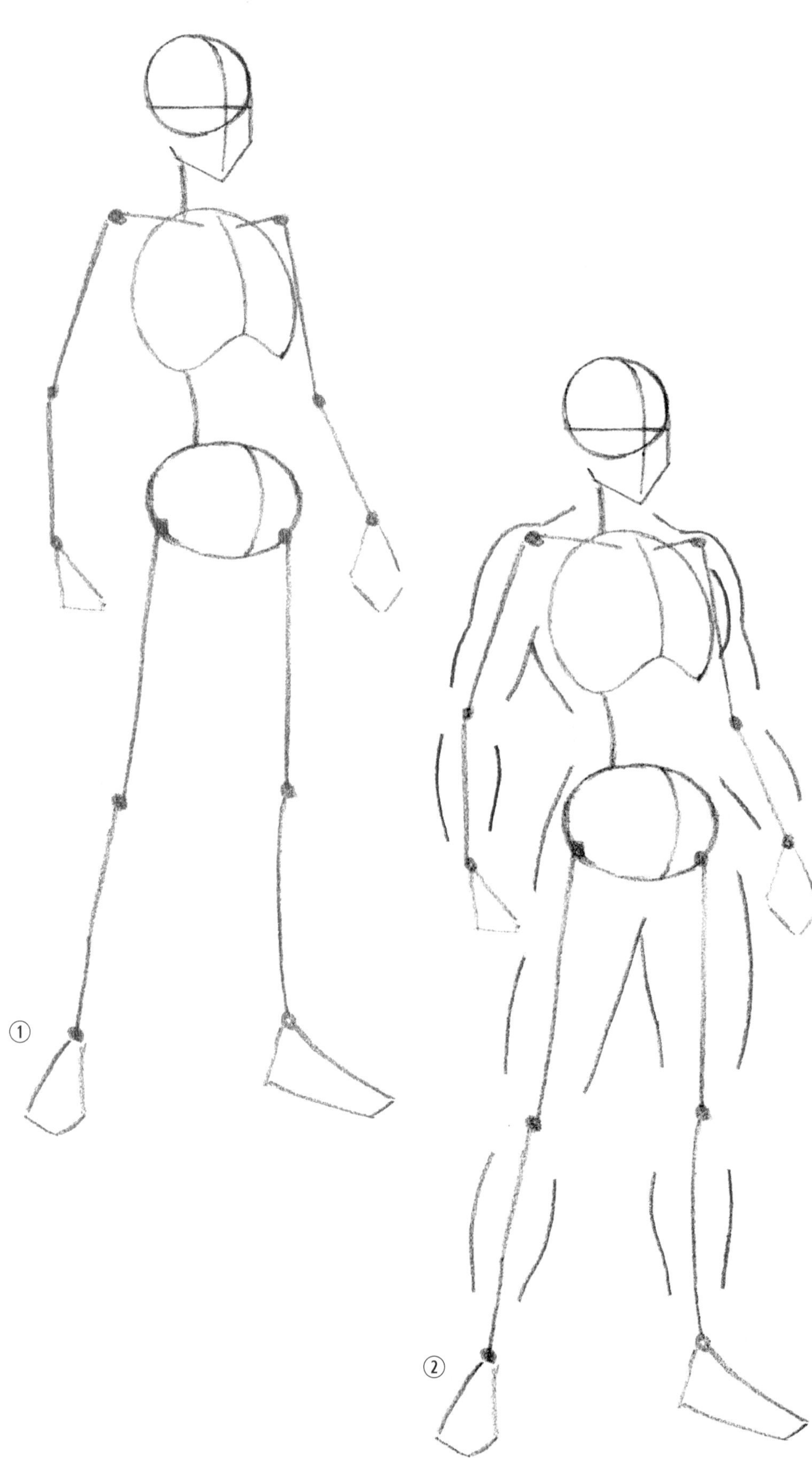

Step 3

Fill in all the gaps around Duke's body outline as shown. When you are drawing a figure at this angle, notice that the line of the neck to the right of your picture is farther from the spine than the other one. The same is true for the waist.

Step 4

Add some more lines to the upper body to define the bone structure and muscle—the muscle diagrams on page 37 will help you to understand what's going on here. Add the hands and feet to your outline, then start to shape the hair and facial features.

>>

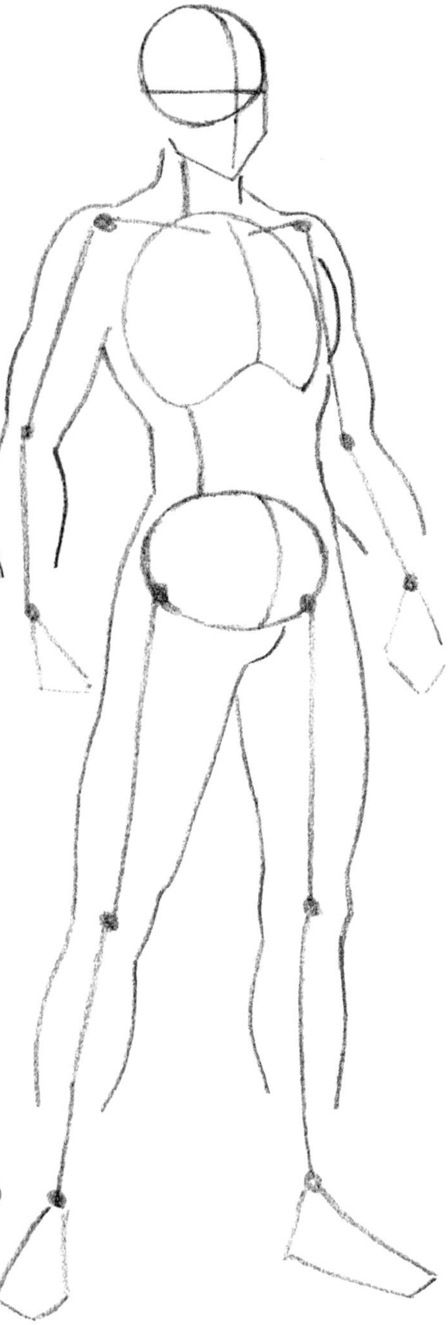

③

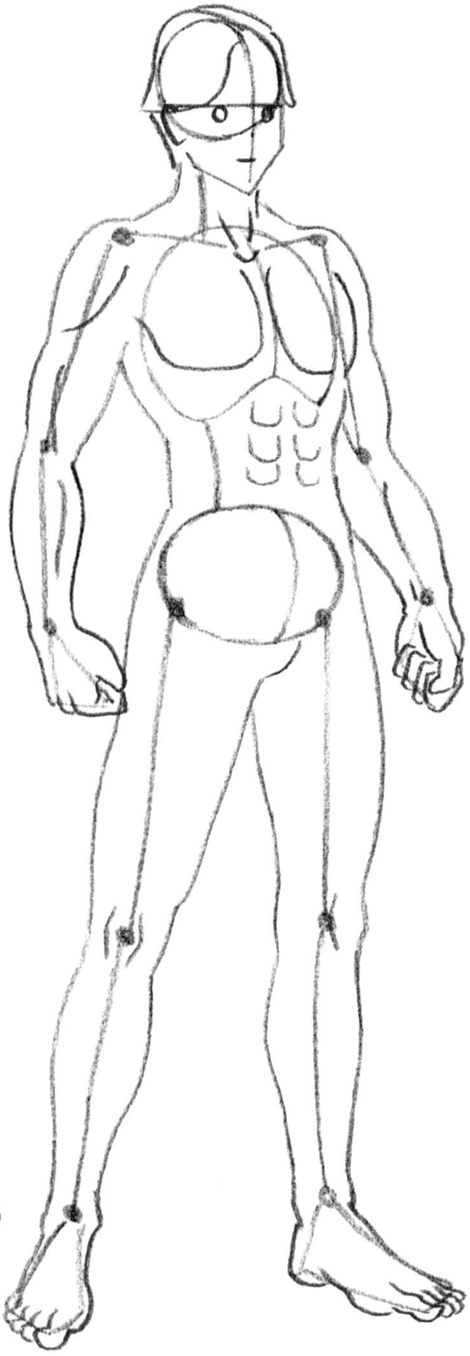

④

«

Step 5

Add Duke's swimming trunks, then go over all the main lines of your drawing in pen, finishing off the final details. Don't forget all the extra little lines on Duke's neck, chest, arms, and legs, as well as on his stomach. Spend some more time on his face, especially the eyes.

Step 6

Once the ink is dry, you can erase the rest of your guidelines.

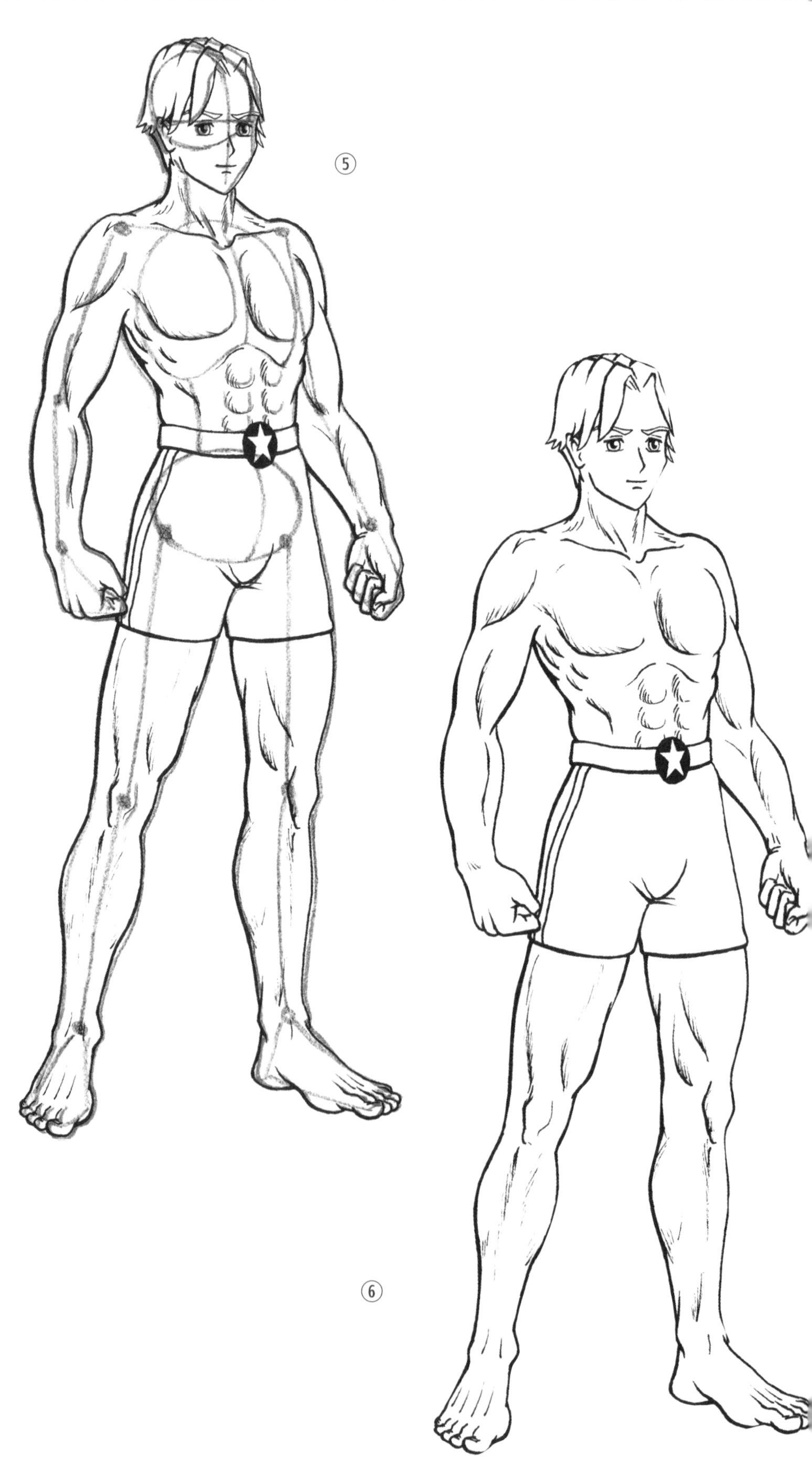

This is quite a sophisticated picture, so if your finished drawing looks anything like this one, you're doing really well. If it hasn't quite worked out, don't worry—that's perfectly normal! Just keep practising.

Hands

Drawing realistic-looking hands is tricky, but well-drawn hands will give your pictures an expert quality. Just like the rest of the body, they can be broken down into basic shapes. Let's start with the back of the hand.

Step 1

Draw a rough outline of the overall hand shape before adding the individual bones—it's a bit like the shape of a fan. Draw a large circle at the bottom of the shape for the wrist. The finger bones and joints all radiate out from this—the bones are the straight lines and the circles are the joints. The thumb should stick out to the left.

Step 2

Now outline the flesh and muscle around the bones. Look at the back of your own right hand to help you.

Step 3

Draw on the fingernails and some little lines to define the knuckles.

Step 4

Erase the lines and your drawing of the back of the hand is complete.

Step 5

To draw the other side of the hand, reverse the drawing you did in steps 1, 2, and 3, then copy all the crease lines you can see here.

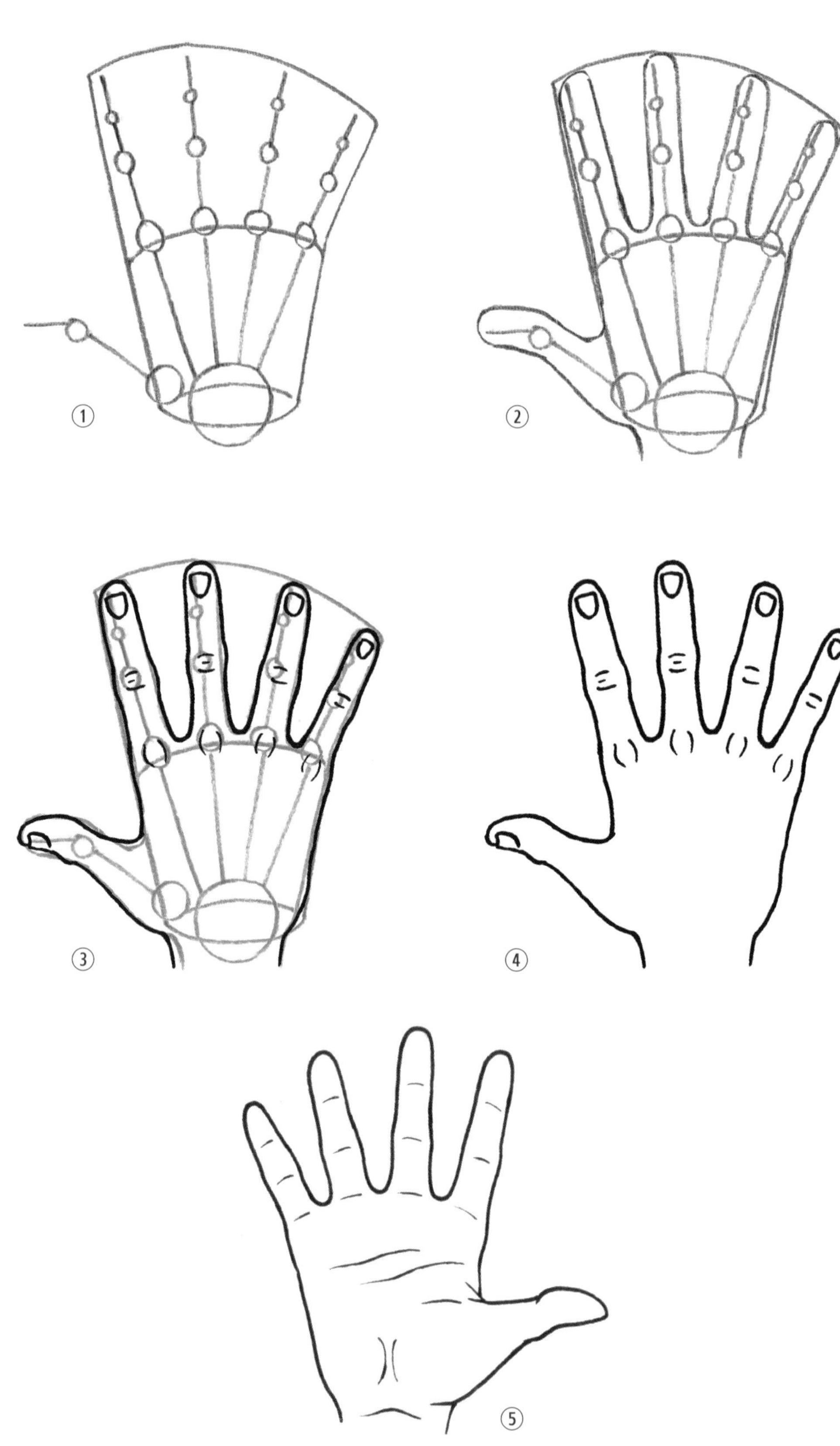

Hands in Action

In manga, hands are used as fists, levers, and counterweights in fighting. They are also used for holding tools and weapons like clubs, swords, guns, and rocks. They can convey a lot about the emotion of a character too.

① Poses

Here are some examples of Duke's hands in action. I've added some guidelines to help you draw them.

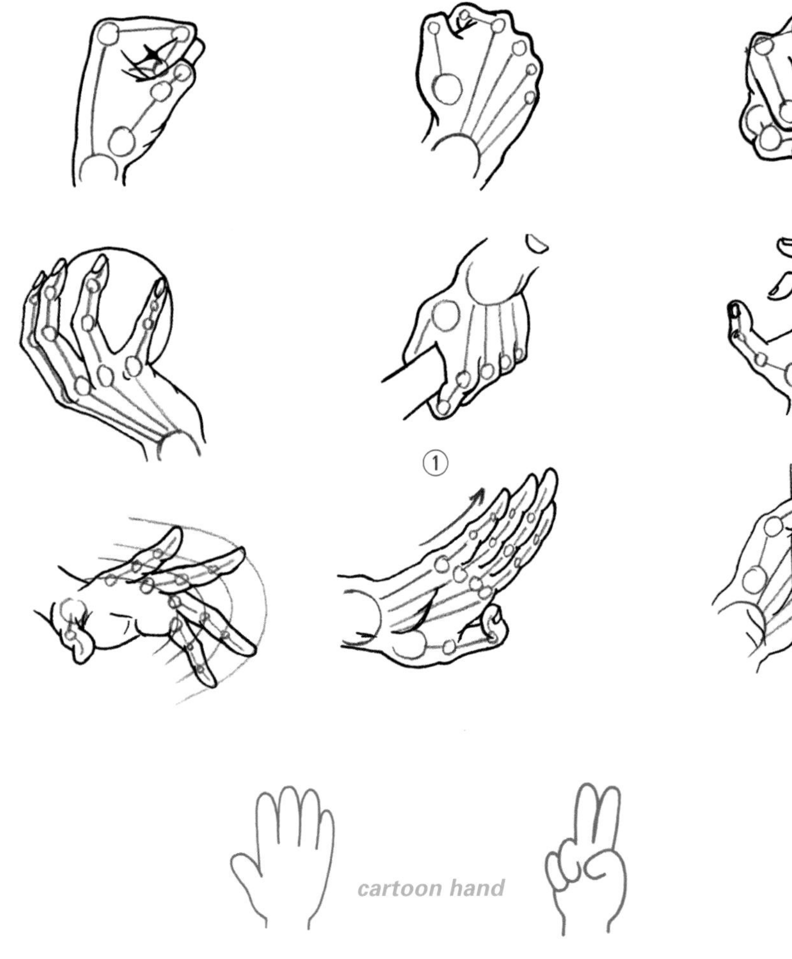

② Simplifying hands

Some artists choose to simplify hands. There are different ways of doing this, but the hands must always look like they belong to the figure you are drawing.

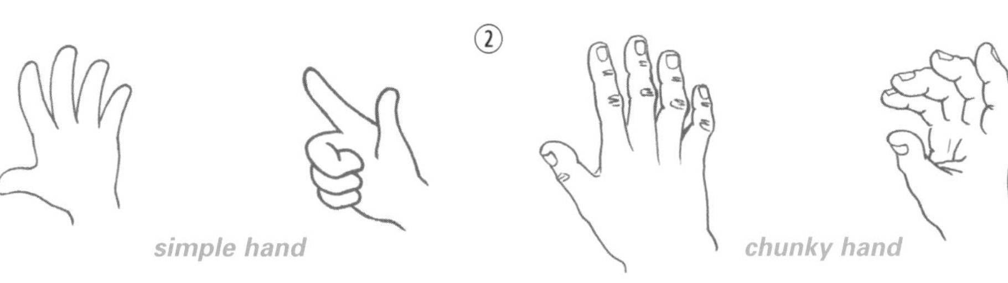

③ Different ages

It's clear that these hands belong to characters that are very different in age. The baby hands are chubby, so the bones and joints aren't very defined. The older hands are much more bony and wrinkled.

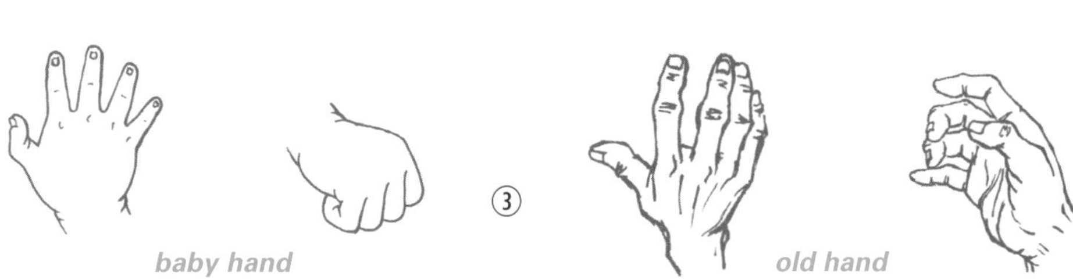

Proportions

Manga artists work out the relative sizes of their characters using head lengths. This is Duke at four different ages. As he gets older, the shape of his body doesn't change as dramatically as that of a manga woman, but there are still important transformations.

① Toddler Duke

This is Duke at about three years old. The younger a character is, the larger his head tends to be in relation to the rest of the body. You can see from the guidelines that Duke's whole height is four times the height of his head. Manga children are much chubbier than manga adults.

② Preteens Duke

At nine years old, Duke is about six heads in height. His chest is becoming broader and he is generally more muscular.

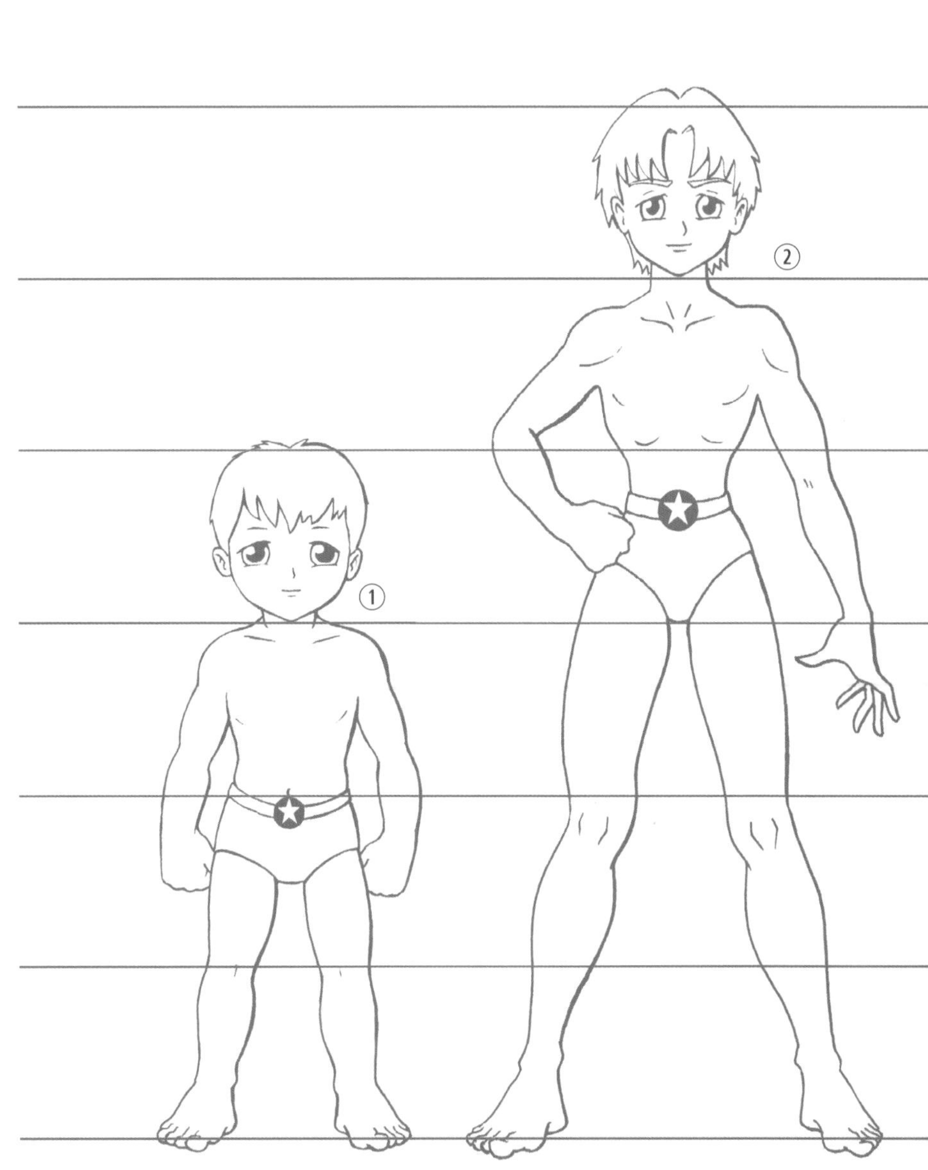

③ Teenage Duke

Duke is now well into his teens, so he is nearly fully grown. His muscles are now well developed. At seven heads in height, Duke is quite tall for his age—as heroes often are. Some manga males are only about this height when they are fully grown adults.

④ Adult Duke

This is Duke at his fully grown adult height of eight heads. Male manga characters can be up to 10 heads tall, but this tends to be the incredibly strong or evil ones. As well as having developed even bigger muscles, Duke has more flesh around the waist, making his chest less defined. His thigh muscles are also larger in relation to the rest of the legs.

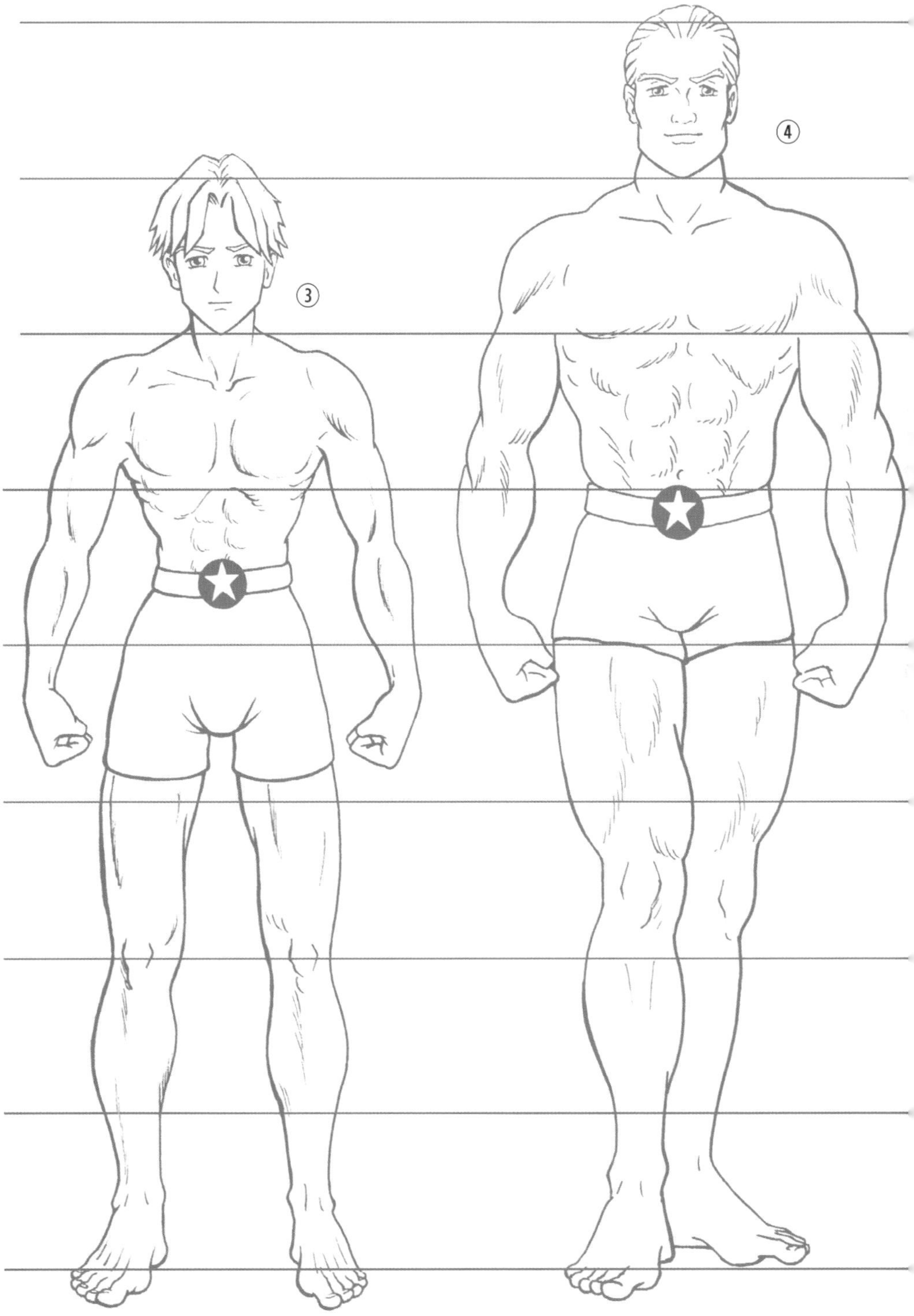

③

④

In this section, we're going to look at inking your drawings, coloring, and applying tone. You'll also learn something about how different colors work together.

Colored pencils are the easiest to use, so you may want to start with them and then move on to felt-tip pens and watercolor paints. Once you start working with paints, you'll want to use thicker paper since this won't buckle when it gets wet.

Experienced artists have their own preference for using certain materials depending on their style and on what they enjoy working with most.

Although adding color can produce fantastic results, it can also ruin a good drawing if the color isn't applied well. Spend some time experimenting with different materials to see how you get on with them, and so you learn about the different effects that can be created with them.

Art materials can be very expensive, but you can get by quite well with just a few. All the examples in this book were done with the kinds of materials you might already have in your own home—so look around before you start spending money!

COLOR
COLOR
COLOR
COLOR
COLOR
COLOR
COLOR
COLOR
COLOR
COLOR
COLOR
COLOR
COLOR
COLOR
COLOR
COLOR
COLOR
COLOR

①

③

⑤

②

④

Light & Shade

Making some parts of your drawing darker by shading them with pencil will create the illusion of solidity and depth. Think of shading as coloring in black and white. Don't get too carried away with your pencil—you should leave plenty of your paper uncovered since the lighter some parts of your picture are in relation to others, the darker and more dramatic the shadowy areas will look.

① Lighting from the side

This is my manga character Min. Here I've shaded him as if the light source is coming from behind his right shoulder. The boy is therefore more brightly lit on the parts of him that face up to the right. The left-hand side and the parts of his body underneath wouldn't receive so much light, so I have shaded them darker.

② Lighting from below

You can use lighting for dramatic effect in your pictures. This time Min is lit from below right, which makes the image look more creepy. The bottom part of Min's face will naturally be better lit than the top and sides—the top and sides should therefore receive the heaviest shading. Use a soft pencil for this.

③-④ Adding backgrounds

When you put each of the drawings of Min you have already shaded against a dark background, the differences become much more obvious. Compare picture 1 with 3 and picture 2 with 4. On the darker edges of the figure I have blended the outlines into the background.

⑤ Block shading

When you have had a lot of practice at visualizing the shading of your drawings, you might like to try block shading in ink or felt-tip pen. The effect can be quite dramatic and is commonly used in manga and other comic styles. It may look simple, but you have to be very confident to get it to look right. Start with a clean drawing that you've outlined using black felt-tip pen, then think very carefully about which areas would be in shadow from a chosen light direction.

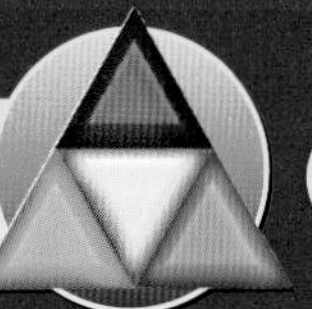

Color Theory

There are a few basic rules to follow when you are using color.

① Primary colors

Red, blue, and yellow are the basic colors that make up all other colors. They are called primary colors, and I've used them for Duke's clothes in picture 1. If you can only afford three colored pencils, pens, or paints, go for these colors.

②–④ Secondary colors

Green, orange, and purple are called secondary colors. Each one is a combination of two primary colors. In pictures 2, 3 and 4, the colors of Duke's pant legs make up the color of his tunic.

⑤ The full spectrum

The three primary and three secondary colors represent the full spectrum of pure bright color as you would see in a rainbow. If you use them all in one drawing, as I have in picture 5, the result can be overpowering, so don't use too many different colors in one picture.

⑥–⑦ Tints and shades

When colors have white added to them, they are called tints and look pale and pastel, like in picture 6. When colors have black in them, they are called shades and look darker, like in picture 7. Using different tints and shades will make your pictures look much more sophisticated.

⑧ Complementary colors

Some colors go better together than others. Every primary color has one secondary color as its complementary color, which is a combination of the other two primaries. So, for instance, red is complemented by green (blue plus yellow). Good combinations can be made by using complementary colors. Picture 8 is created using various tints and shades of yellow and purple (red plus blue).

⑨ Harmonious color schemes

In picture 9, a harmonious color scheme has been created for Duke's clothes by using just blue—it has been turned into different tints and shades by adding white or black.

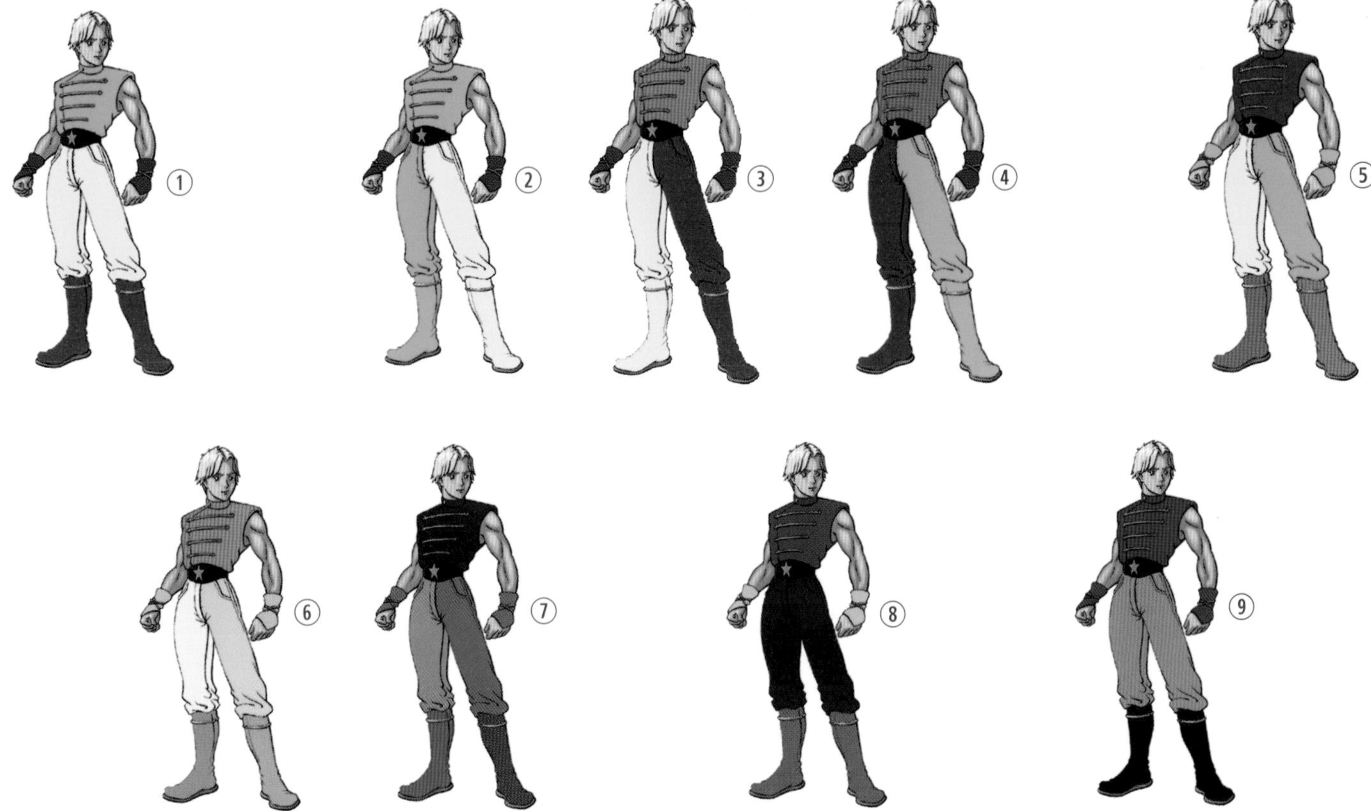

Inking & Coloring

I made a sketch of Min, photocopied it several times, then finished it in several ways, using different materials and different kinds of shading and color.

① Pencil

Here I've shaded my sketch of Min using pencil. In some parts, the shading is lighter than it is in other areas because it is shaded as if he is lit from above left. You need not always use black pen for outlines; pencils alone can produce pleasing and subtle artwork.

② Simple pen line

Here I've outlined my original sketch of Min using a fine-tipped black pen—the kind that you can buy quite cheaply at any art or stationery store. This is fine as a basic outline but it will need a lot more work before it is in manga-style and captures that distinctive flavor.

③ Finished pen line

Traditionally, manga artists use a pen with a metal point, which they dip into a bottle of black ink. This produces lines of varying thickness, depending on how hard the pen is pressed against the paper, but it can be tricky and messy to use. A simpler, and more controllable, effect can be achieved by retracing the simple ink line, varying the width of the lines to accentuate curves and darkening the edges which face away from the light source.

④ **Colored pencils**

Once you've made a good solid outline of your picture, you can experiment with finishing it in different ways. Although colored pencils will not give you really professional results, they are easy to use and can look convincing if you use them wisely. The colors can be blended to create new ones. I've done this here by working one color over the top of another. The pencils are especially good for quickly sketching new color schemes in rough, even if you then choose to apply color to your actual picture using different materials.

⑤ **Felt-tip pens**

For this picture I used colored felt-tip pens. These produce vibrant results very quickly, and are particularly handy since you can get them in a vast range of colors. I used felt-tip pens of artist's quality for this exercise, but they are very expensive—you can achieve similar results with the cheaper variety.

⑥ **Digital color**

The color has been added to this picture on a computer. You can find out more about computer coloring later in this section. If you have access to a computer, you will probably enjoy coloring this way. If you don't have a computer, don't worry—manga artists were producing beautiful artwork years before home computers were invented.

Computer Coloring

The computer is the favorite method of coloring manga artwork, especially among younger artists working in the style. The process can take a while to master completely, but the principles are quite straightforward. Various software packages are available for the purpose. To follow the exercise I'm going to show you next, you'll need Adobe Photoshop, one of the most common packages.

Scanning and preparation

Before you can start coloring, you have to convert your drawing into a digital file for the computer. To get the best result, set the scanner to a high resolution—say, 500 dpi—and choose the grayscale option. This will give you sharper lines to work with later. When the image is open in Photoshop, reduce the resolution to 300 dpi. This is about the maximum you'll need to print with; higher resolutions will slow down your computer.

Now convert the image (in Image>Mode>) to RGB (Red/Green/Blue) to allow you to start using color. At this point it's a good idea to look at your work close up and clean up any obvious blemishes. Don't be too fussy about this—as long as you sort out the major imperfections the small ones won't catch the eye. Use the Eraser tool for this.

Making sure your background color is white, choose Select All (Apple or Ctrl + A) and then New Layer Via Cut (Apple or Ctrl + Shift + J). Set the Blending Mode of this layer to Multiply, name it Line Art, and then lock it with the Lock icon. You shouldn't need to touch your original artwork again.

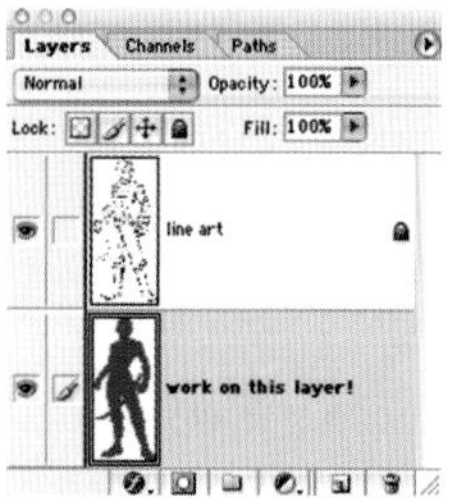

Hint: I use an Apple Macintosh computer, for which the command key is labeled with an Apple symbol. If you use a P.C. the same function is achieved with the control key labeled 'ctrl'.

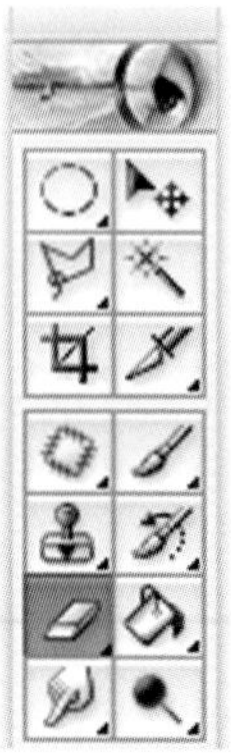

Eraser

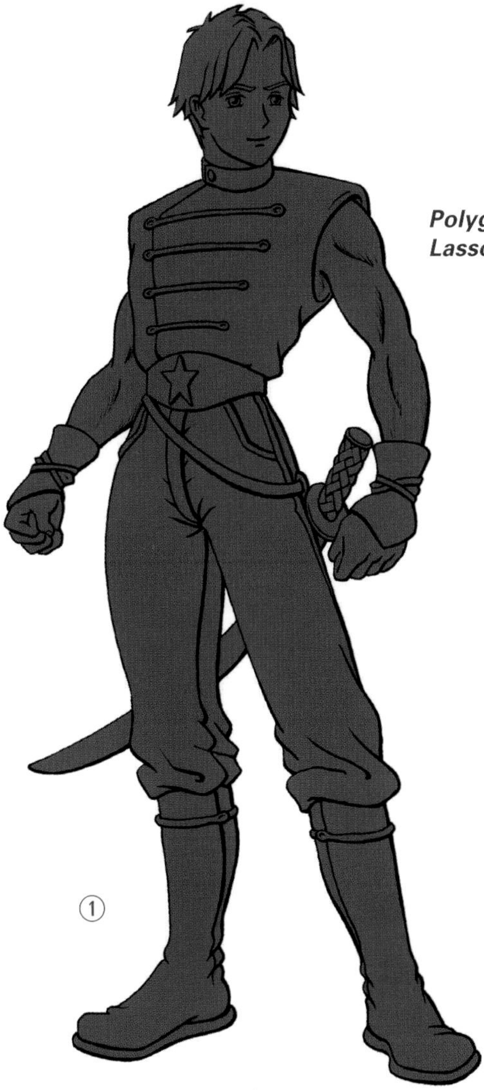

① First color

Apply the color (termed Flat Color) on the layer below that of your original line artwork. Begin with the color that covers the largest area of your figure—in our example it's Duke's pants. I'm using a medium gray for them. You have to apply this color to your entire figure in order to separate the figure from the background. In further steps we'll change different areas to other colors. To apply the gray, first magnify your image, then use the Polygon Lasso tool to select the area. Now fill up the image using the Bucket tool.

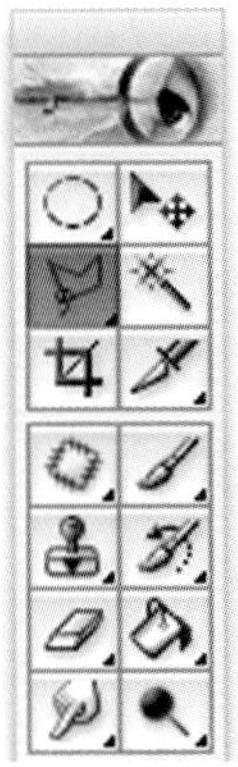

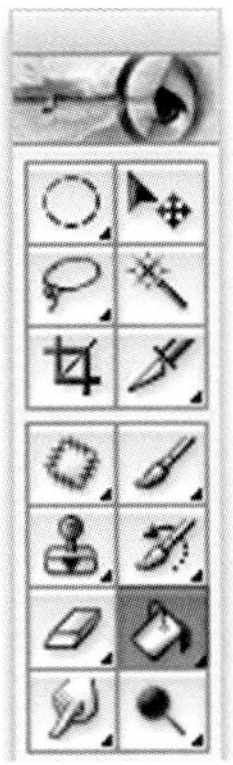

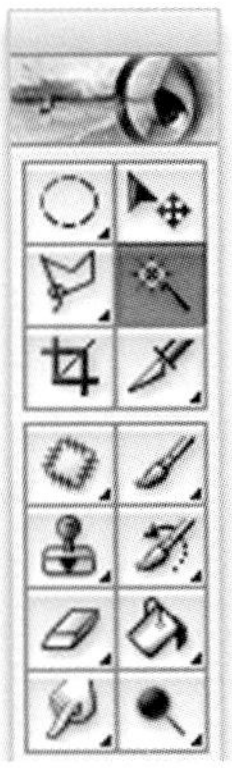

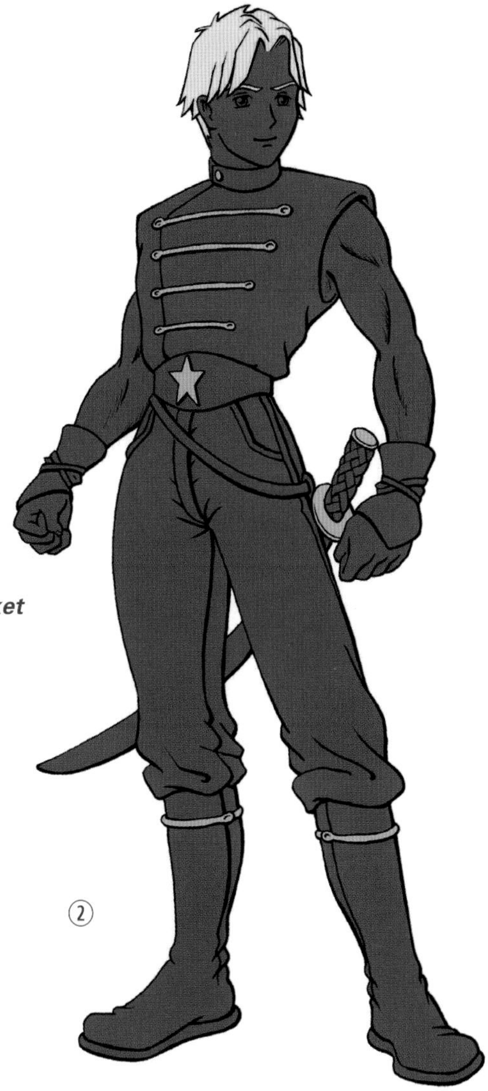

② More colors

Now you need to change the parts of your figure that are taken up with other colors. I could've selected the second largest area, the tunic, but I've chosen for our example to show you what you do when the same color crops up in several distinct areas of your figure. Here it's the gold of Duke's hair, and eyebrows, and the details on his tunic and boots. Once more, use the Polygon Lasso tool, and fill the area using the Bucket. Or, change the color using Image > Adjustments > Hue/Saturation (Apple + U). Repeat this process with the other colors—see how many you can pick out apart from Duke's tunic, and his boots. Hint: Each time you draw out your rough selection area, you can use the Magic Wand with the Alt key pressed down to deselect any differently colored areas that you may have included accidentally.

③ Saving the flat color

Once you've got all the flat color down, select New Layer Via Copy to copy the layer. Name the new copy of the layer (which will appear at the bottom) Flat Color, then lock it. You shouldn't need to change this layer again, but it will prove useful when you're working with the Magic Wand tool later. You should have been saving your work regularly, but save now if you haven't already.

④ Adding shadows

It's time to add some shadows. For this part of the exercise, we'll be using Quick Mask. Click on the Quick Mask icon or press Q. Using the Brush tool, paint an area you want to show in shadow. Don't worry if you go over the lines—we'll tidy up later. Hint: To make Quick Mask easier to use, double-click on the icon in the tool palette to view its Options palette. Check Color Indicates: Selected Area and choose a dark mask color. To see what you've just done, leave Quick Mask mode (press Q again or the icon in the tool palette). You'll see that you've selected an area of the image. For a more feathered selection you can use a softer brush. Now you can clean up the selection by going to your Flat Color layer and using Alt plus the Magic Wand tool as you did earlier.

Go back to your working layer (the middle one) and use Image > Adjustments > Hue/Saturation to shade to your taste, or just fill it up with the Bucket tool.

③

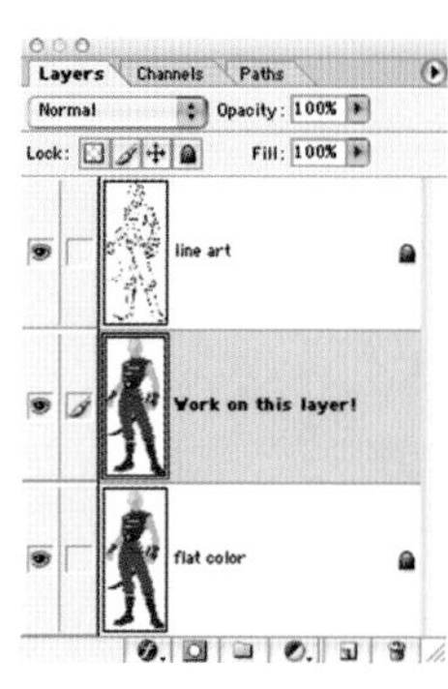

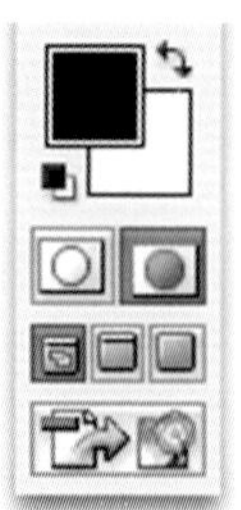

Quick Mask

④

⑤ Highlights

You can use the same technique you used for the shading to make well-defined areas of light and dark. This is how I worked on Duke's hair.

Hint: If you would like precise control over the area of highlight, you can instead magnify the image and use the Lasso tool to select the shapes you want. For most of the images in this book, I used the Dodge tool, which softly lightens colors wherever it is applied. If you prefer a more painterly style of shading, you can use it and the Magic Wand to mask off the areas you're working on.

Your work should now be ready to print out.

Dodge

⑤

Drawing action figures that look really convincing is all about capturing the shape and movement of the character's body.

To get these right, you will need to increase your awareness of the body and how it behaves, so to help you do this, we'll be studying some new poses and we'll take a look at perspective. I'll also introduce you to the technique of foreshortening, which you'll find a useful skill for enhancing your pictures, and making them look more realistic.

There are plenty of opportunities in this section for you to put theory into practice to create some great action characters, male and female. To draw them, it is more important than ever that you start with light pencil lines. If you do this you'll be able to keep resketching until you get them absolutely right—don't be afraid to keep changing your lines until they look accurate.

Persistence does pay off in the world of manga, as the characters you'll be meeting next will demonstrate. If you want results, you have to get going, so let's move it!

ACTION
ACTION
ACTION
ACTION
ACTION
ACTION
ACTION
ACTION
ACTION
ACTION
ACTION
ACTION
ACTION
ACTION
ACTION
ACTION
ACTION
ACTION

Action Poses

The pose of the body conveys mood, movement, and personality. All of these examples are based on distinct human emotions and show clearly what each character is feeling despite the absence of the facial features. The figures look realistic because they only bend in the same way that a real person's body bends. Shoulders, wrists, and ankles can swivel in many directions, for instance, but knees and elbows can't bend backward or sideways. Remember this when you create poses.

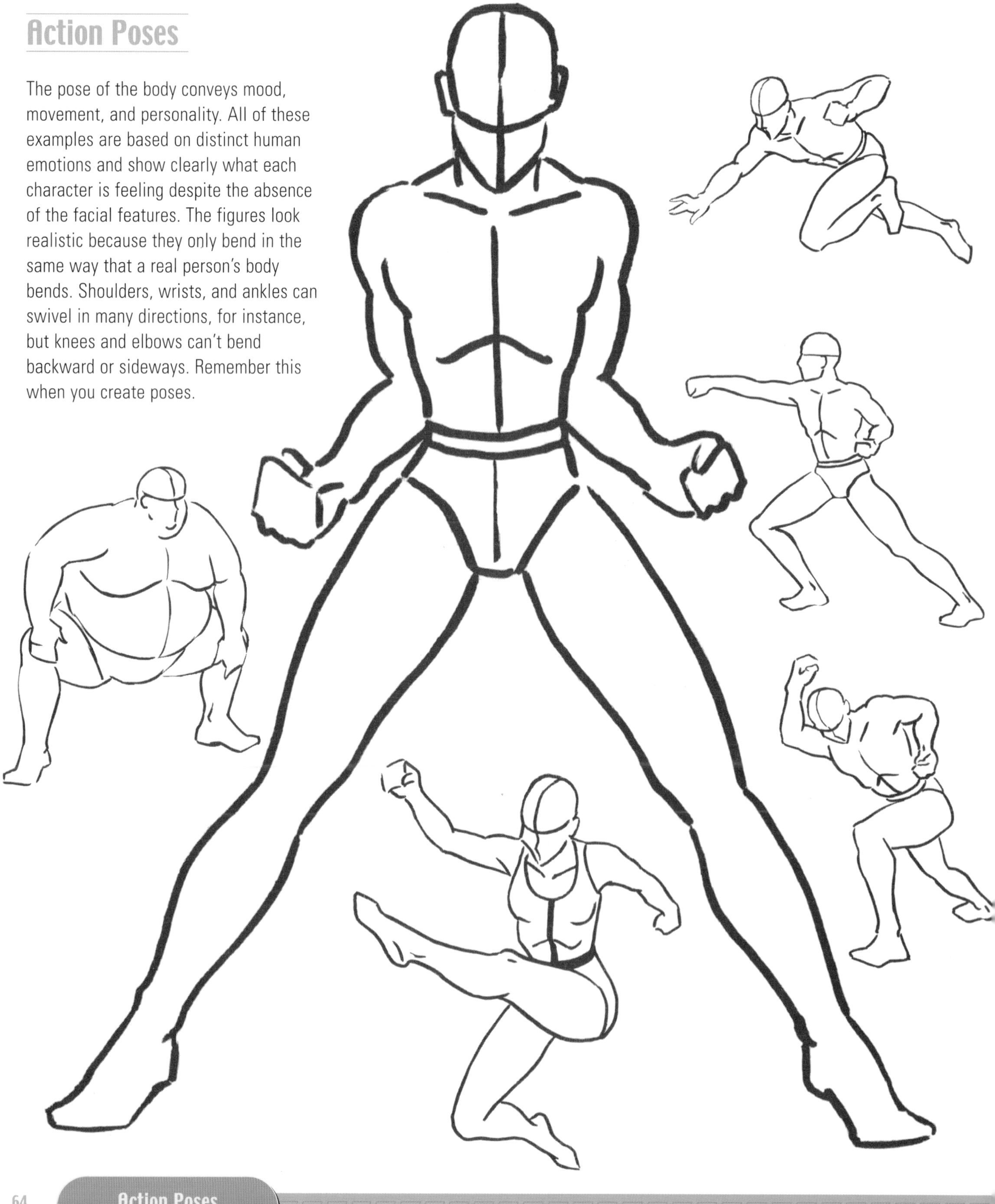

Copy these action stances for practice, then come up with some of your own. Use your own body to try making a pose you want to draw so that you can see if it's really possible!

Triumphant Warrior

In this exercise, we're going to draw a fully clothed, dramatically posed action character named Treen. The drawing involves a lot of the aspects we've covered so far, like expression, pose, muscle build, and dynamic hands. Take your time with each step.

Step 1

Draw the skeleton framework as shown. Make sure you copy the central lines on the body parts carefully since these will help you get the rest of the detail in the right place. Look at how the position of the arms affects the shape of the shoulders too.

Step 2

Now that you've had some practice drawing Duke's body, you should be able to draw all the shapes of the flesh in one stage. A lot of the body is going to be covered by clothing, but roughing out the shape will help you to draw the clothes. Copy the red lines as accurately as possible. Notice that Treen is much more heavily muscled than Duke.

①

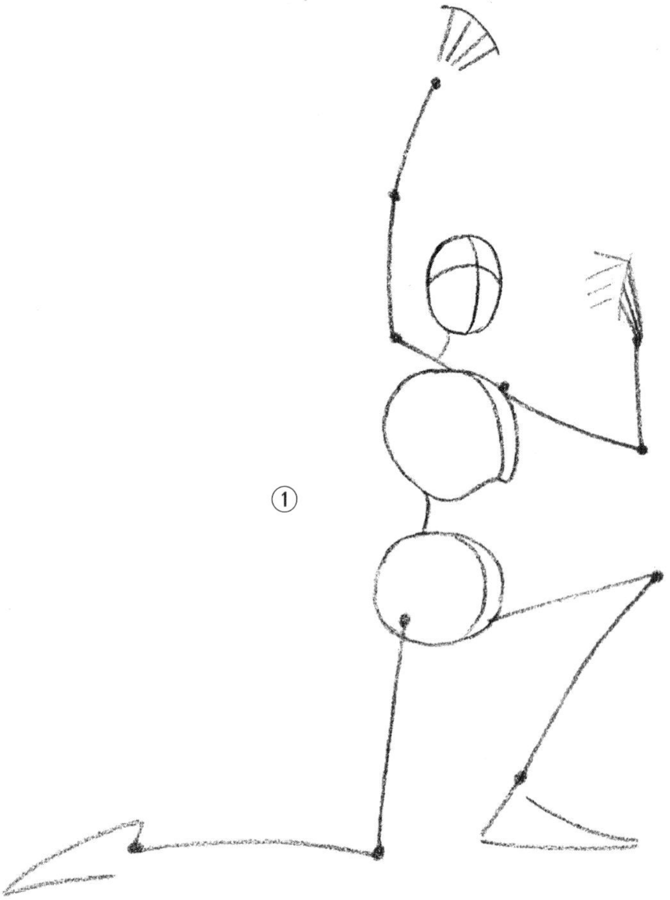

②

Step 3

Still using light guidelines, rough in the approximate shapes of the clothing and sword. Do some more work on the hands, then start placing the facial features. When you outline the hair, try to capture the way it looks when it has been caught by a gust of wind. The waistcoat too should be drawn with a similar texture to suggest fur.

Step 4

Now for some of the detail that really makes this triumphant stance. There's a lot to think about here—the facial expression, the rest of the outline for the hair and clothes, and the strapping around the legs and wrist. Notice the fold lines on the pant legs.

>>

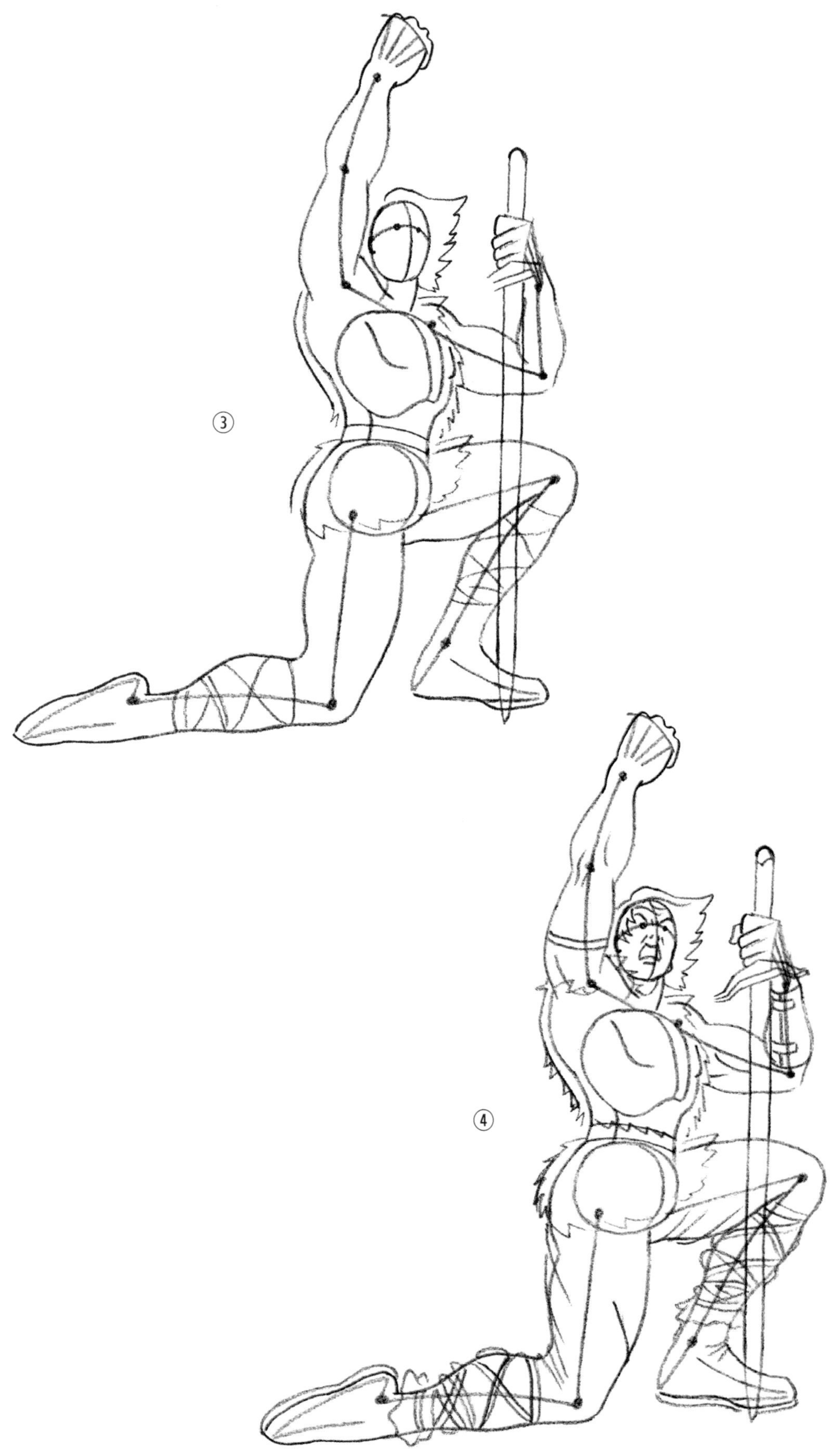

<<

Step 5

Now that all the main guidelines forming your picture are in place, you can enjoy going over all your good lines in ink. There are all sorts of features you can add here—finish off the face and hair, add more detail to the handle of the sword, and work on bringing out the texture of the fur. Copy the fold lines on the boots, and the definition on the backs of the hands.

Step 6

When the ink is dry, erase the rest of your pencil lines to leave a clean picture.

⑤

⑥

You can copy this color scheme to complete your drawing or use different colors and patterns. You might then want to draw the figure again but add different details of your own. The clothing style could change, or you could put a different expression on Treen's face. You could make the arms slimmer or more muscular.

Juni the Sorceress

The main thing to notice about the pose of Juni is that it's not balanced. If you tried to stand like this yourself, you would fall over. That imbalance, as well as her hair and clothing, gives the impression of movement. Take a look at the finished picture of her on the last page of this sequence before you start.

Step 1

The slight twist in Juni's waist affects the positioning and shape of the hips in relation to the head and chest, so copy these parts carefully. Only one foot is lightly touching the floor, while the other is poised to bound forward. Notice the pose of the arms and hands too.

Step 2

Now you need to add the body outline to your skeleton framework. Juni's muscles are toned and taut, but not bulky like a man's. The curves on her raised arm show the softness of her young skin.

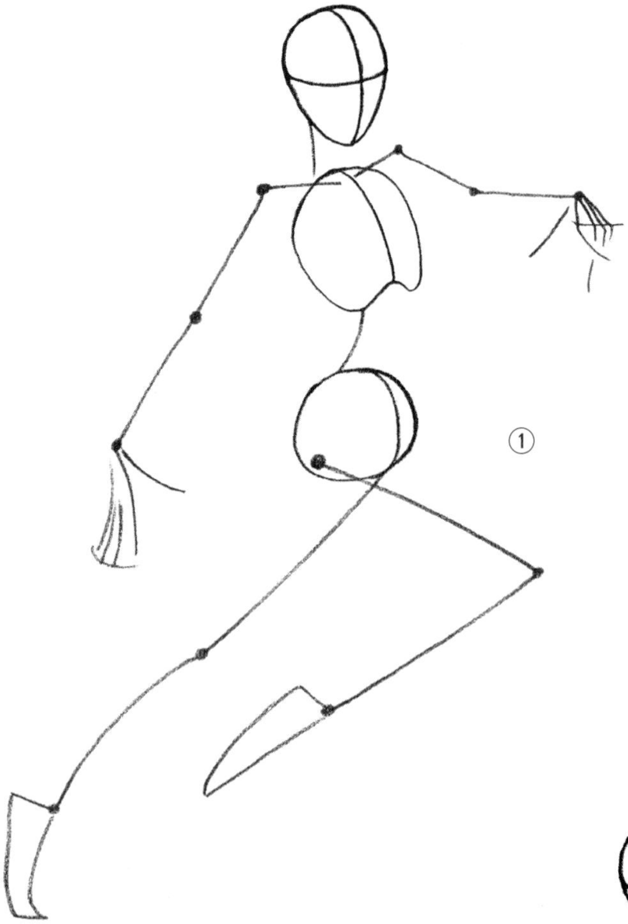

①

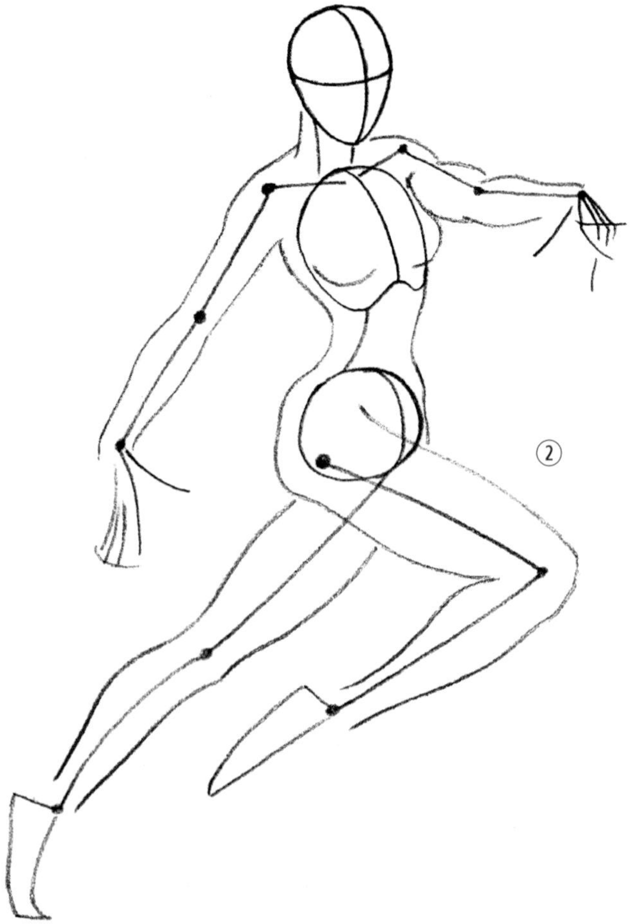

②

Step 3

Roughly draw in the clothing. The hair and skirt flow backward, adding to the sense of movement. The wavy hair falls away from a center part. The skirt radiates out from a gathered waistband. Work on the fingers of the hands here too and outline the feet of the boots.

Step 4

Now for more detail. Work on the gentle look of the facial features and draw the curls of the hair. Add the tops of the boots, including the crisscross lines of the laces that fasten them. Use the same technique for the front of the bodice. Putting some bangles on one of the wrists as shown will add to the sense of movement.

③

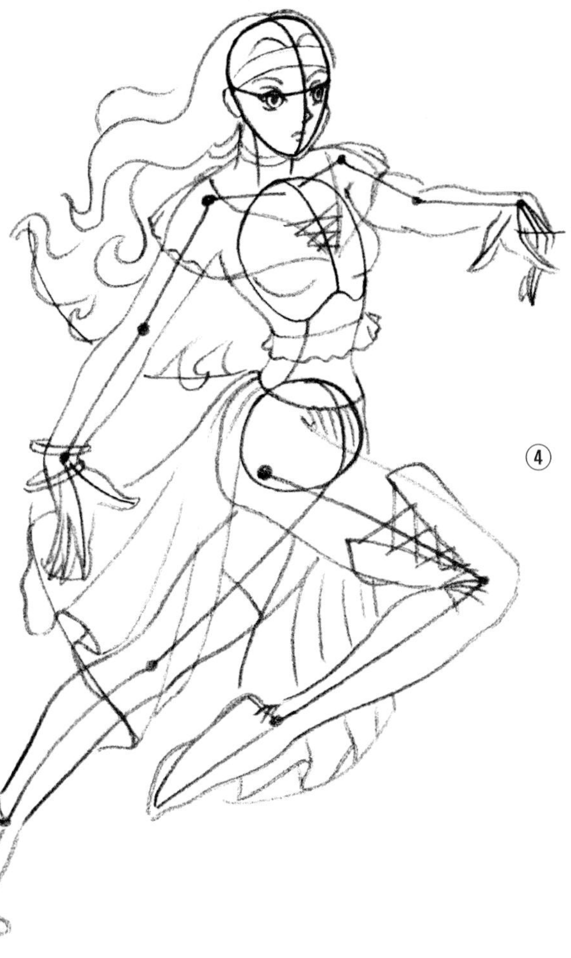

④

«

Step 5

Now you should be ready to pick out the final lines of your drawing and go over them in ink. Notice the extra little gather lines I've added around the edge of the collar on the bodice, and the curves I've used to outline the shape of the chest. Draw some short curves along the center part too. Don't forget the belly button.

Step 6

At the last minute, I decided to draw a flame generating from Juni's finger to show that she has special powers—it's not too late to add details like this. When the ink is dry, erase any remaining pencil lines.

⑤

⑥

Adding color will really bring your character to life here. The hair is almost black underneath, where it's in the shadow of the thick locks flowing over it.

Basic Perspective

① Eye level

This figure is viewed from the level of the hips as shown by the horizontal line in green—this is known as the eye line or horizon. Features above this line, like the elbows and shoulders, appear to slope downward as they get farther away from us, even though they are really level. Features below our eye line, like the knees and ankles, slope the other way. The farther above or below our eye line the features are, the steeper the angle of the slope.

②–③ Changing eye level

In picture 2, our eye line is much higher, whereas in picture 3 it is much lower. Notice how this affects the degree to which different parts of the body slope.

④–⑥ Different views

Here I've used some fully formed figures to help you further understand perspective. When we are looking down on a figure, as in picture 4, we can see more of the top of the head and shoulders, and less of the legs. When we look up at the figure, as in picture 6, the opposite is true. In all of these pictures, the horizontal green line shows the level from which the figure is viewed.

①

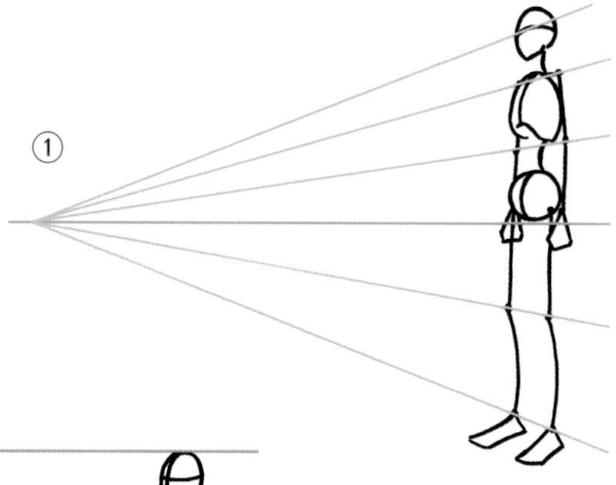

②

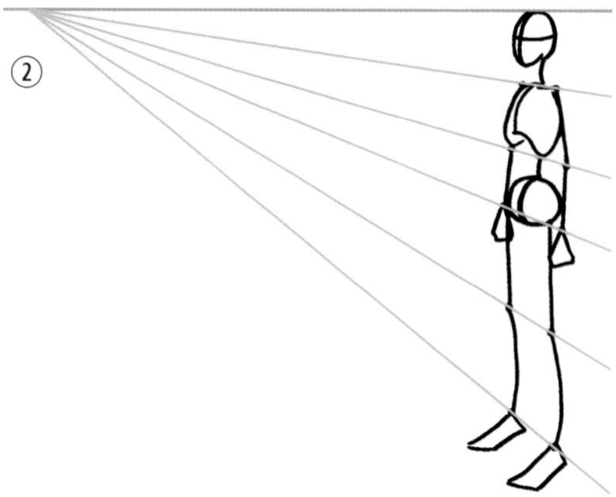

③

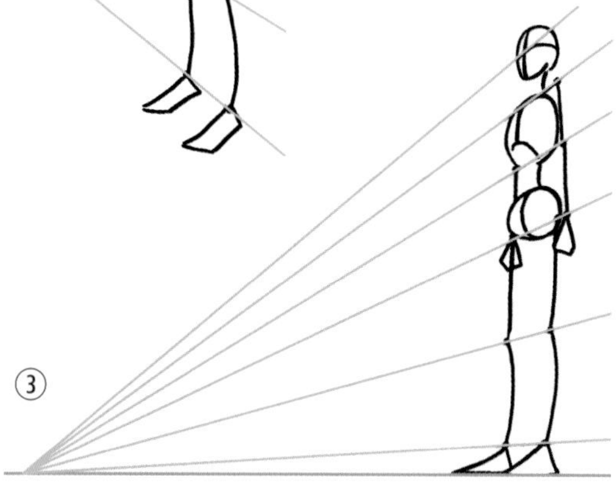

④

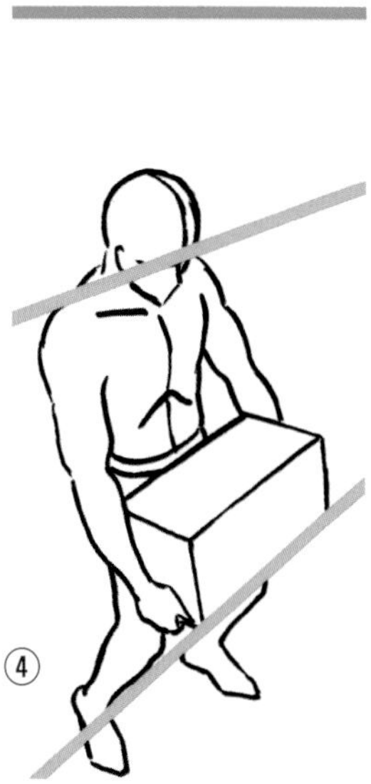

⑤

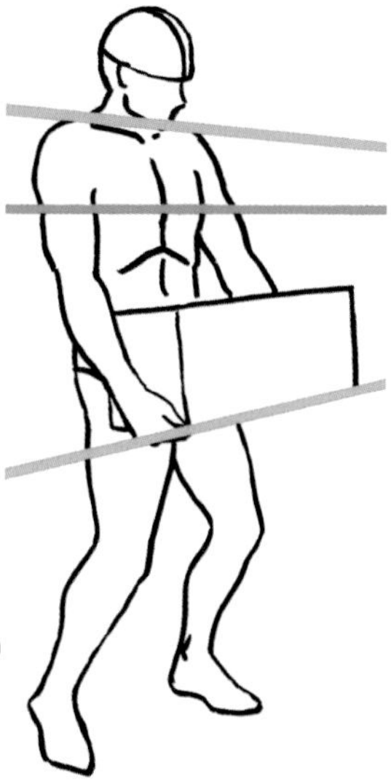

⑥

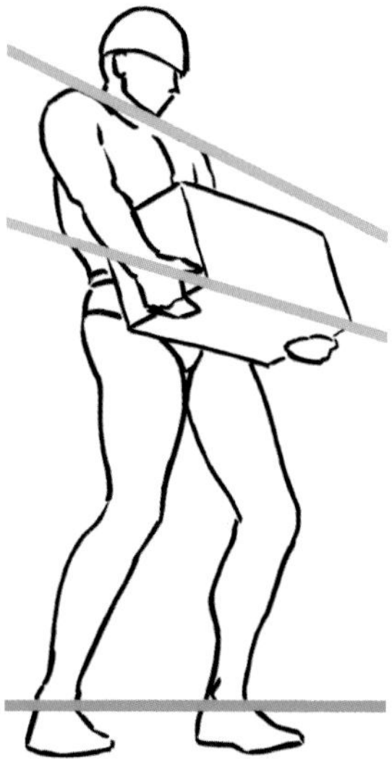

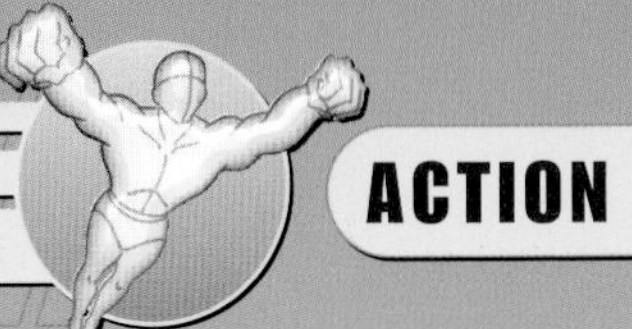

Foreshortening

Another technique that is used to make manga figures look more dynamic is foreshortening. This is when the parts of a figure that point toward us look shorter than the parts we see from the side. This can be confusing to draw but can give a picture real impact.

① Side view

Picture 1 shows a flying figure drawn from the side. The lengths of the torso, arm, and leg are all in proportion to each other, but the picture lacks dynamism.

②–④ Changing proportions

If we draw the same pose from a different angle so that it tilts toward us, as in pictures 2, 3, and 4, the figure looks much more dynamic. If you look closely at these pictures, you will see that the proportions of the various body parts have changed. The arms have been shortened, the hands enlarged, and the legs and feet made smaller. Although these proportions aren't really correct, the figure looks normal because the oversized parts just look like they are closer to us and the reduced parts look as if they are farther away.

The more the relative proportions are exaggerated, as in figure 2, the closer the figure will seem to us. The less the distinction between the large and small features, as in picture 4, the farther away the figure will seem.

①

②

③

④

Advanced Perspective

When we draw the human body, we have to take into account the fact that it is not flat. Like all solid objects, it has more than one plane (surface). The simplest way to think of this is in terms of cubes.

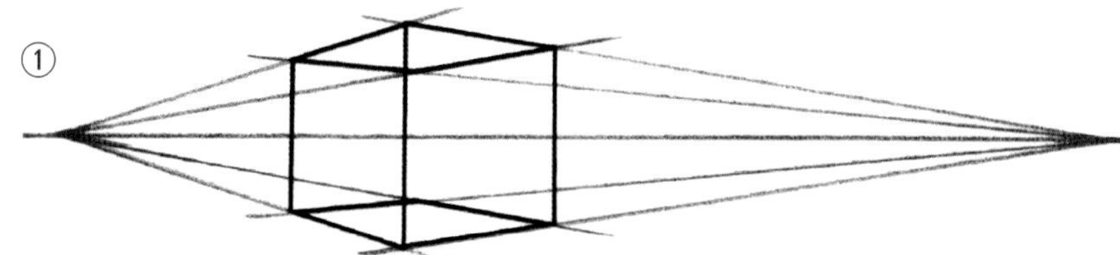

①–③ Vanishing points

The surfaces of this cube all face away from us but in different ways. You can see that their lines all recede toward the horizon, meeting at two different points along it—these are called vanishing points. Notice how moving these vanishing points changes the angle of the cube. It's the same for any object.

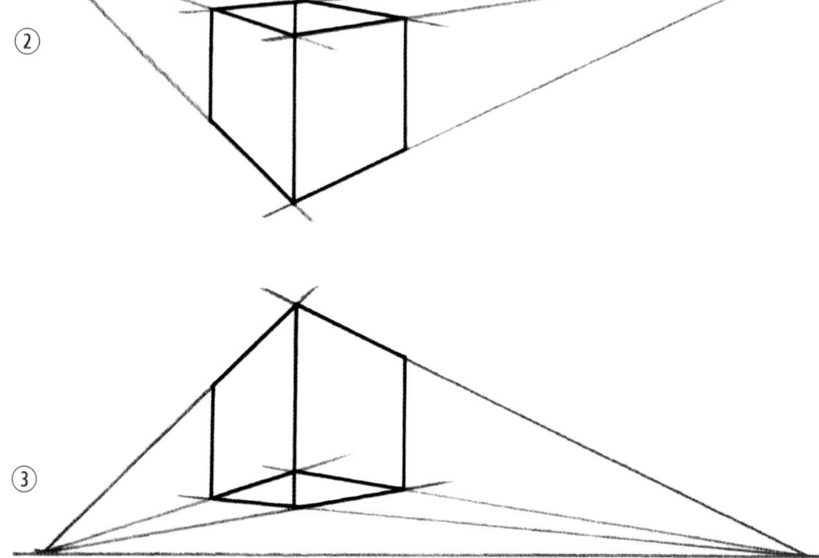

④ Stacking cubes

If we stack the cubes on top of each other, we have a shape that will help us draw a three-dimensional figure in perspective.

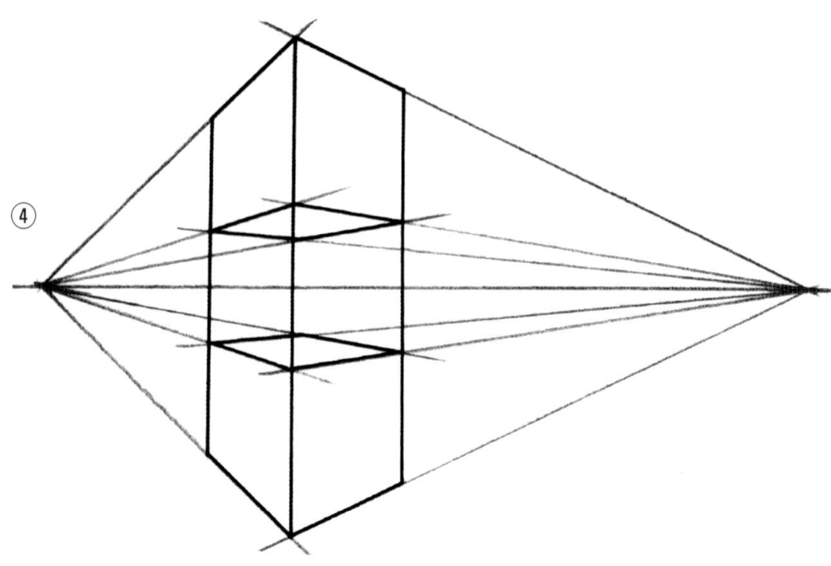

Figures in Perspective

Let's stack up some boxes that have rectangular faces to make a larger shape that will help us to draw Duke in perspective.

① Front view

This is Duke as we have drawn him already, straight on from the front. This is a good angle to learn about drawing the proportions and muscles of the body, but it doesn't really bring Duke to life.

② Turning the boxes

Here I've turned the boxes so that they are at a ¾ viewpoint. If Duke stands at this angle, you would be able to see the front and the side of his body, but if we just draw his front and side views on the sides of the boxes, he doesn't look very realistic.

③ Thinking in 3-D

To draw Duke at this angle, we need to think three-dimensionally and imagine him standing inside the shape—understanding how the lines forming the edges of the stacked boxes recede above and below the eye line allows us to visualize the angles of Duke's body.

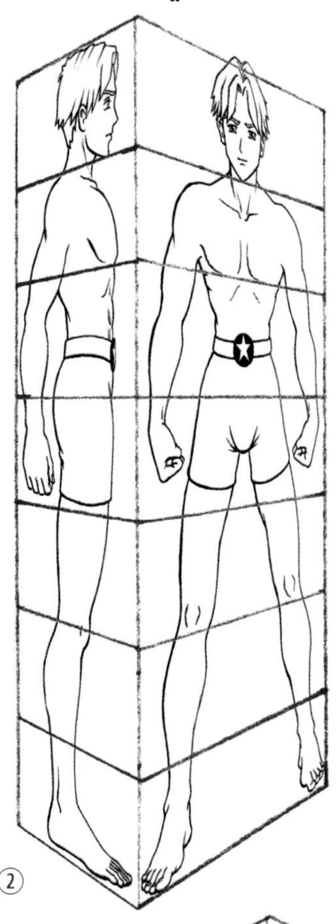

②

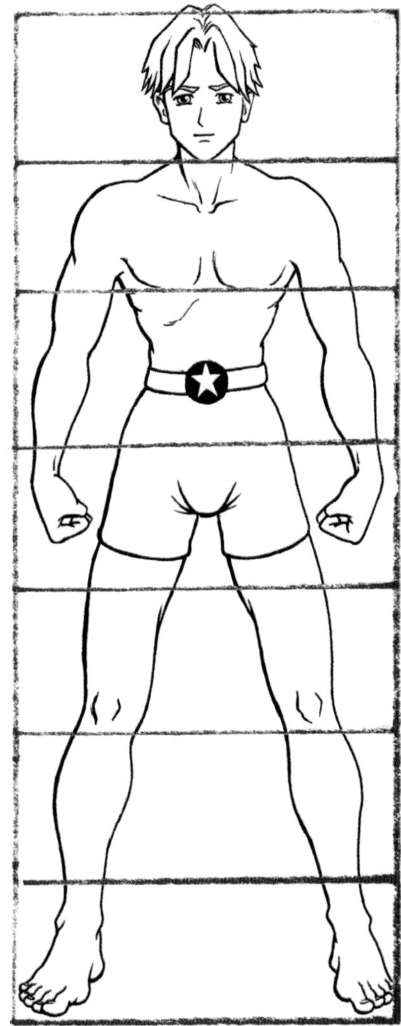

①

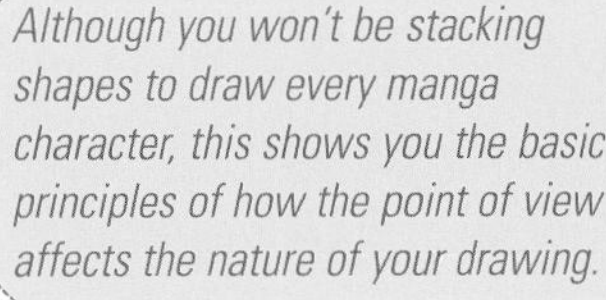

Although you won't be stacking shapes to draw every manga character, this shows you the basic principles of how the point of view affects the nature of your drawing.

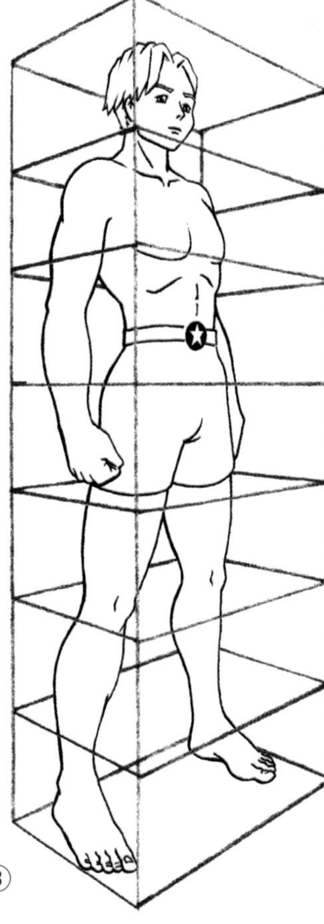

③

Throwing Boy

Now that you've learned some of the theory about perspective, let's try putting it into practice. Bear in mind that this young character, Kom, is viewed from a very low eye line—level with his ankles.

Step 1

I've drawn on the receding lines to help you with the perspective. Start by drawing the main body parts as shown, then add the limbs. Notice how from this perspective the joints of one arm sit higher than the joints of the opposite arm, as highlighted by the receding lines. When you draw the legs, the ankle joints should line up horizontally. Notice how the knee joints don't both sit on the receding line here since one leg is positioned farther back than the other one. The outlines for the feet should be quite large. Add the ball above Kom's head.

Step 2

If you've drawn your skeleton framework accurately, adding the outline shape for the flesh and muscle here should be easy. Kom is only a boy, so his muscles aren't very well developed yet. You can place the eyes at this stage, too.

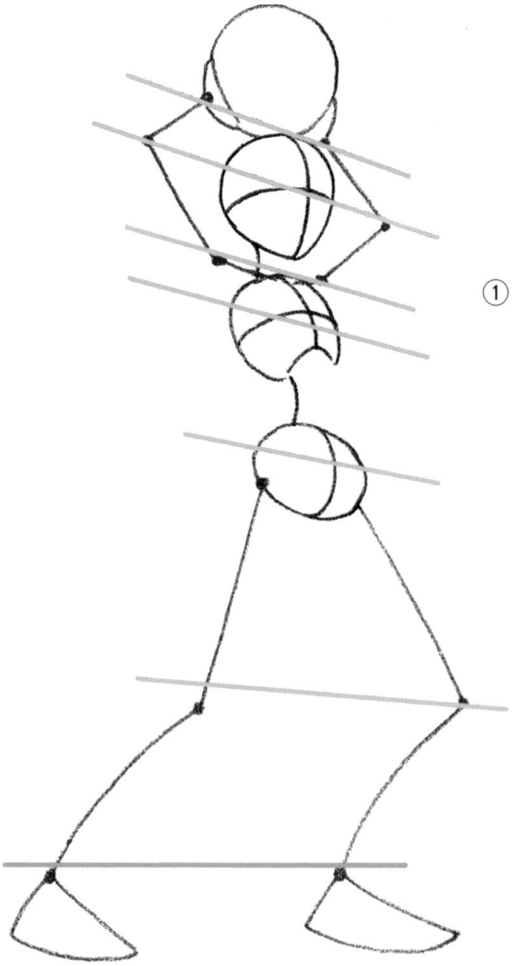

①

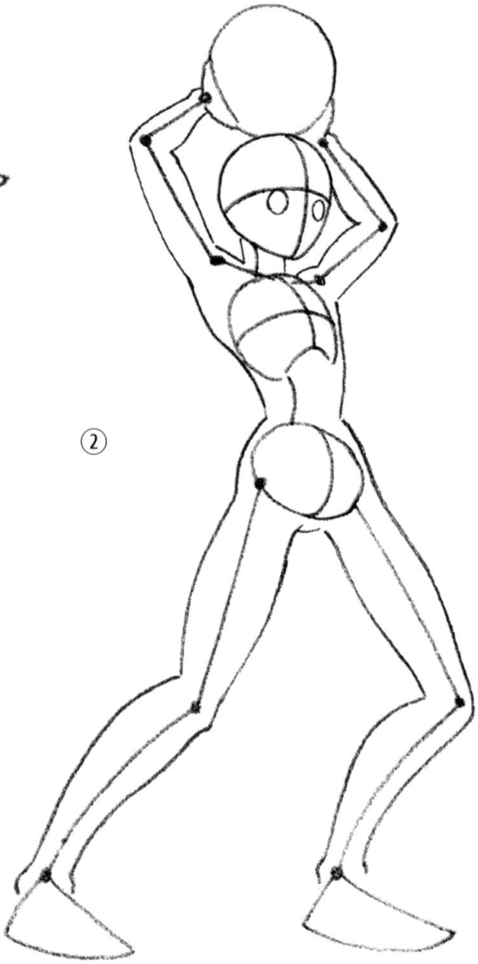

②

Step 3

Start sketching in the clothing. Notice how the legs of the boots are large and angular. Remember that we are looking up at Kom, and he is also leaning backward slightly, so the shins and feet are drawn bigger so that they appear closer to us. Next place the rest of the facial features and the hair.

Step 4

Now for more detail. Work on the hair and eyes, then add all the lines that show the ribbing on Kom's space suit and boots.

>>

>>

Step 5

Go over your drawing in pen. By adding some detail to the ball, you can change its texture and turn it from a soccer ball into a lump of rock from outer space. Add some crease lines to the backs of the knees too.

Step 6

When you have erased the remaining pencil lines, your space boy drawing is finished.

⑤

⑥

Use some space-age colors like these to make Kom look really futuristic. You could add a symbol to one of his leg guards, like I have, to show the clan he belongs to. Notice how the space rock casts a glow across the top of Kom's head and the insides of his arms.

Karate Girl

Let's apply the idea of foreshortening to a drawing of manga action girl Jenna, who is practising karate.

Step 1

Start by drawing the three main body parts. Take the time to position them accurately since everything else hinges on them. Next attach the limbs—copy the proportions of them as they are drawn here. The back arm should be shorter than the front one, with a smaller hand. The front leg will have an oversized foot attached to it.

Step 2

Now draw the outline for the flesh and muscles. Notice how the front leg appears broader than the back one. Place the eyes too—Jenna is looking down toward her front foot.

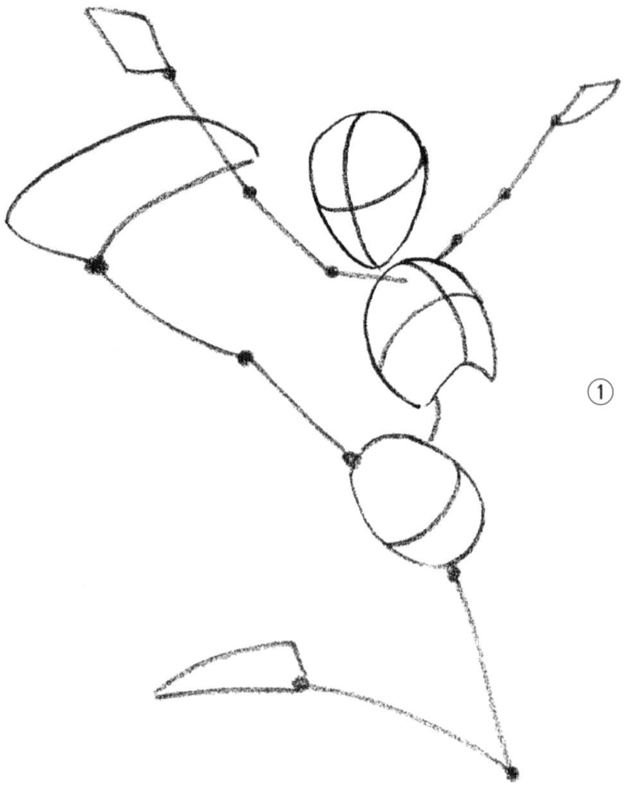

①

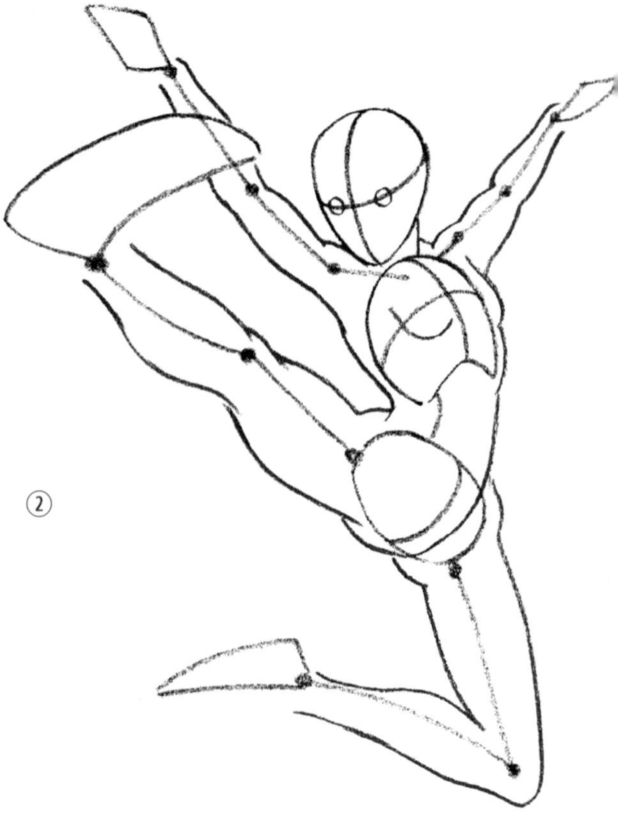

②

Step 3

Sketching in the clothing won't cause you too much trouble if you follow the outline of the body, but notice that the suit is quite loose-fitting so it won't curve in around the joints. Draw the hair flying up behind the head. Place the rest of the facial features too. Spend some time on the hands—try holding your own hands in the same kind of karate pose so you can study the positions of the fingers.

Step 4

From this angle we can see the underside of the shoe on the raised foot—draw some lines across it to show the texture of the rubber sole. Add some crease lines to the clothes—look at your own clothing to see how fabric folds when you bend your arms and legs or twist your body. Work on the hair and eyes as well.

>>

③

④

>>

Step 5

Use a pen to go over the lines that form your final drawing. Give the hair and face more detail and add some lines to the palm of the hand. Don't forget to draw around the ankle bones to define these.

Step 6

When the ink is dry, erase all the lines of your skeleton framework to leave a clean picture.

⑤

⑥

In the final color drawing the drama of Jenna's flying leap is underlined by the shadows and highlights. Notice where the light hits her body, and the way the subtle use of lights and darks emphasizes movement just as much as the actual pose.

PROJECTS

The exercises in this final section will show you how to draw two manga characters in poses that require you to use lots of the different techniques you've learnt about in this book. They will be the most advanced manga drawings you've tackled so far.

The poses complement each other. This offers an additional extra if you ensure that you draw the two figures on the same piece of paper. Once you've drawn both of them, you'll have the beginnings of an action scene.

While you are working through the stages of sketching the characters, don't be afraid to look back at the other sections of this book. They are in the book for this purpose, to enable you to refresh your memory whenever you feel you need to be reminded about a particular aspect of drawing.

If your sketches get really messy and there are still lots of marks left behind after you have erased all the pencil lines at the end, make a tracing of your picture on a clean sheet of paper before you add the color. This will ensure you have a clear black outline to work with, and make the process much easier.

PROJECTS
PROJECTS
PROJECTS
PROJECTS
PROJECTS
PROJECTS
PROJECTS
PROJECTS
PROJECTS
PROJECTS
PROJECTS
PROJECTS
PROJECTS
PROJECTS
PROJECTS
PROJECTS
PROJECTS
PROJECTS

Fighting Hero

Our hero Rik is set to throw a punch at a villain. It's not just his clenched fist that tells us this—it's his whole pose, including the expression on his face.

Step 1

Rik has swung back his arm, ready to land his punch. As he has done so, his whole torso has twisted. Bear this in mind when you are drawing the body shapes—the head and hips are side on while the large chest is at a ¾ viewpoint. The foreshortening is such that the forearm of the fist pointing toward us is very short, so I won't even draw a bone for this. The hand that's about to throw the punch is much larger than the other one to make it look closer to us and more powerful. Notice that the lines forming the bones of the back leg are slightly shorter than those of the front one to make it look farther away. The back foot is raised to show that Rik is ready to swing forward.

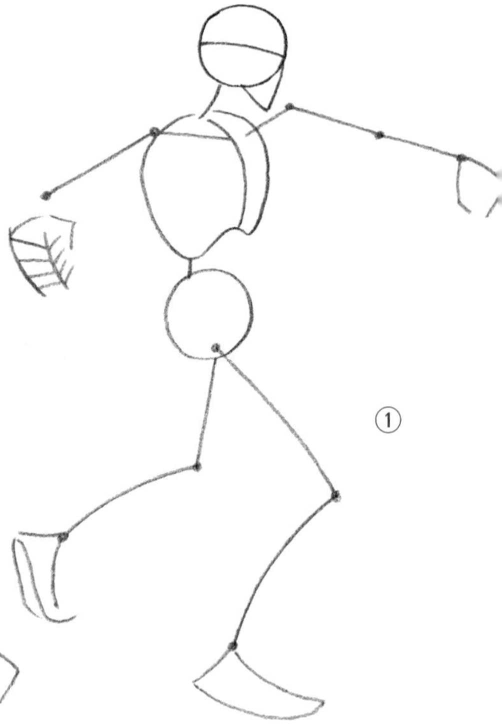

Step 2

Add the body outline. Notice how I've used lots of overlapping curved lines along the arms to emphasize the strong muscles—you can just make out the forearm attached to the clenched fist now. The waist appears very slender, which helps to exaggerate the width of the chest.

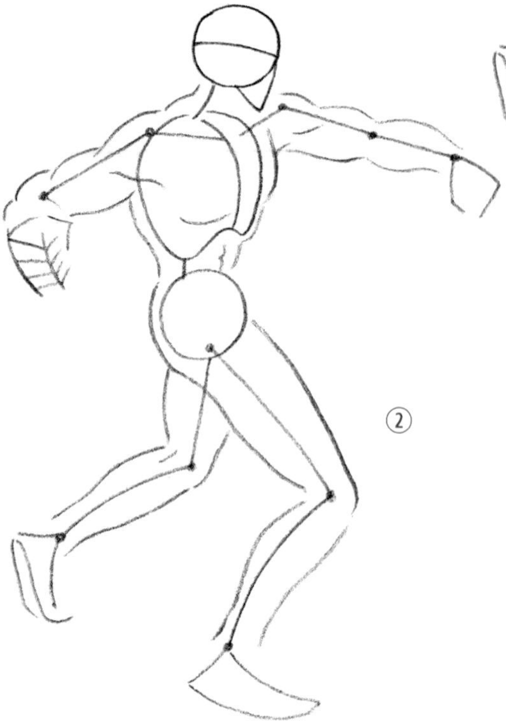

①

②

Step 3

Draw on the outline of the undershirt, belt, and sneakers. It might help you to study the final picture on the next page as you do this. Next add the outline for the hair and work on the facial features. Shape the hands—see if you can capture the drama of the clenched fist.

Step 4

Add some more lines to the hair to emphasize the way it flies up at the back. Draw on the taut neck muscles. Now work on the clothes again—notice how I've added some fold lines to the back of the undershirt and where the jeans bunch up over the sneakers. Copy how the jeans are ripped around the bottoms and across the knee. Draw some lines on the hands to show bandages across the fingers.

Step 5

Now go over the final lines of your drawing with a pen. Don't forget all the crease lines on the clothes and the extra little lines on the body that emphasize bone or muscle. Add any other finishing touches like the tread you can see where Rik has started to lift his back foot. Work on the seamlines that run down the sides of the pant legs—notice how they sit differently where the cloth gathers.

>>

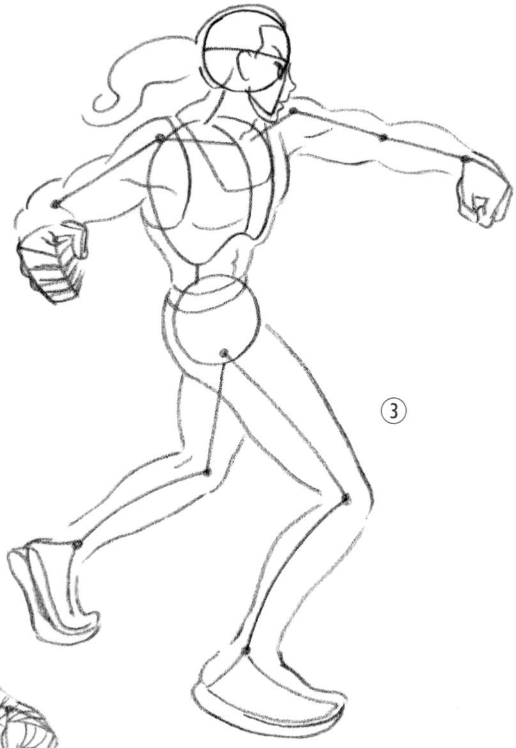

③

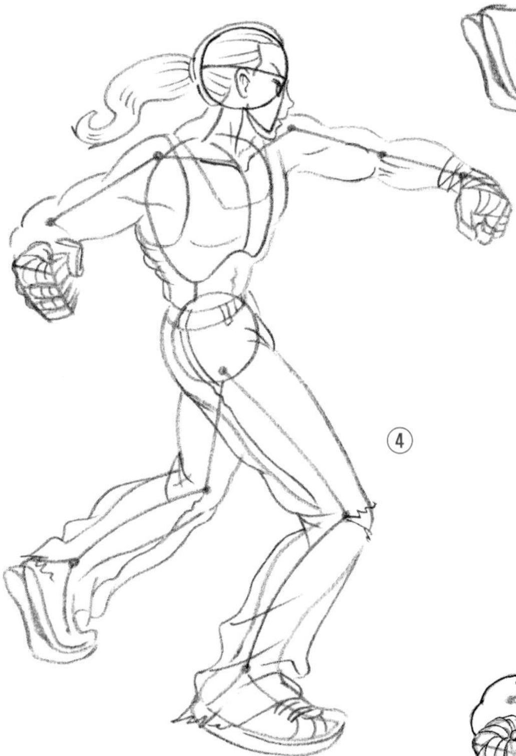

④

⑤

«

Step 6

Go over your final drawing in black felt-tip pen. When the ink is dry, erase all the pencil guidelines that formed your original framework.

Step 7

I've added an extra black line around the neck and armhole of the undershirt to create a band that I could make a different color. I've colored Rik digitally, but you can use whatever method you want.

Step 8

I've imagined that Rik is lit from the direction in which he is looking. Notice how this puts some parts of his body in shadow, like the side of his torso and the backs of the legs. The back of his neck and the shoulder nearer us are in the shadow of his hair.

Finally, I've added the highlights for full dramatic effect. Putting these in so the final drawing has maximum impact takes a sublety of touch that only experience teaches. The only sure way of achieving it is by repetition—so keep on practising!

Falling Villain

This is Steel, the villain who was on the receiving end of the punch being thrown by our hero Rik in the previous exercise. The size of that punch has clearly left him the worse for wear.

Step 1

Start with the three main body parts as usual. Notice how the head is tipped back slightly, making the neck of the spine arch in a different direction from how it does at the waist. Add the limbs—the outstretched hand and foot have been exaggerated in size to show that these are nearer to us and to make the pose more dramatic. You won't need to draw the back foot since this will be tucked under the outstretched leg. The bones that make the framework for the hand will form a wide span.

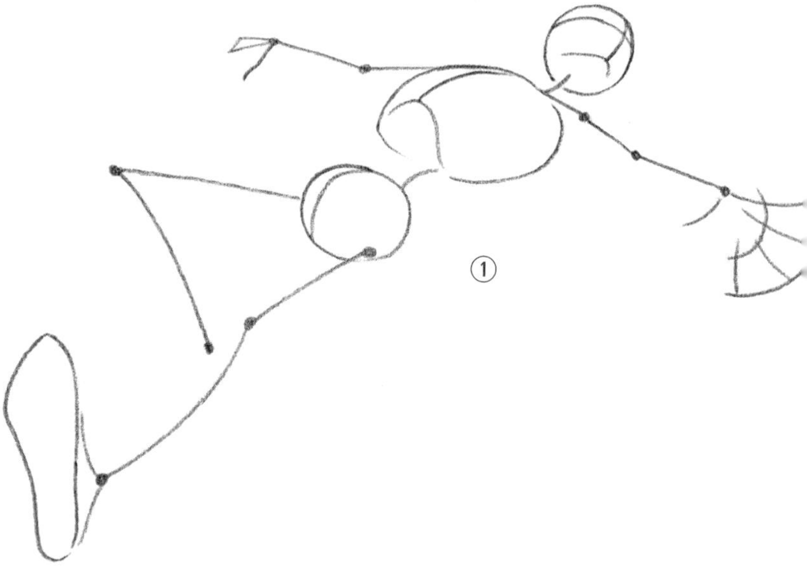

Step 2

Add the outline of the flesh and muscle. Getting this right will help you place the clothes accurately.

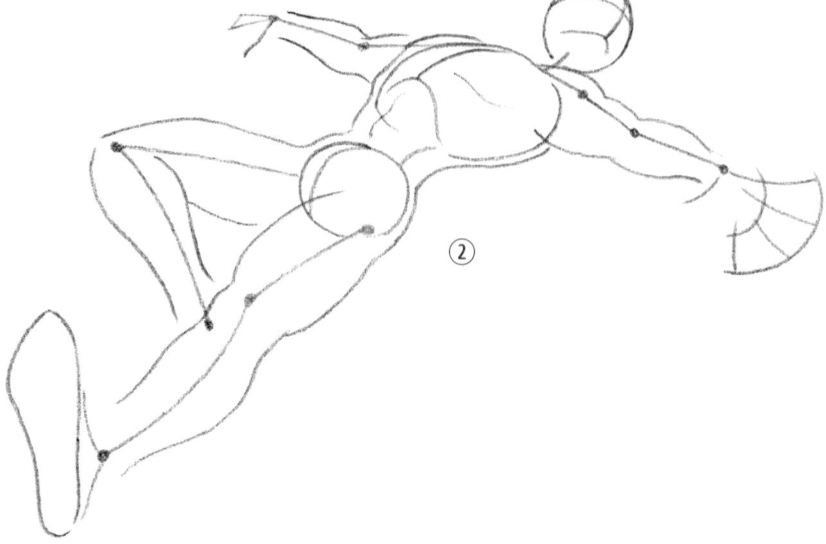

①

②

Step 3

Now for the basic outline of the clothes. Copy the curves of Steel's coat to show the way it has fallen open. Outline the bottom of the pants and the shoe. Next work on the hands. Add the outline shape for the hair and facial features—we're looking at the face from underneath, so we can see only the bottom of the nose. The eyes and mouth must show that our villain is in great pain.

Step 4

Add more detail to the coat—copy the way the collar is partly turned up. Fill in the missing parts of the outline for the pants—draw plenty of fold lines where the back leg is bent. Sketch the jagged outline of the hair, then draw some curved guidelines to the right of the head to mark the position for some blood spouting from Steel's mouth.

Step 5

Go over the best lines of your figure. Add the droplets of blood. Work on the shirt buttons and finish off the belt. Make sure you haven't missed anything, like the detail on the shoe.
>>

③

④

⑤

«

Step 6

When the ink is dry, erase all the lines of your basic skeleton and any other pencil lines you still need to get rid of.

Step 7

Now put in some color to add even more drama to your picture. I've done this digitally, but you can do it by hand, if you choose. If you have drawn Steel and Rik on the same piece of paper, make sure you use the same coloring materials for both figures to create a unified image. Think too about how the colors of their clothing and skin work together.

Step 8

With the flat color in place we can look at adding in the shadows and how light and dark tones can be used to emphasize the pose, underlining Steel's discomfort.

⑥

⑦

⑧

The addition of the highlights focuses our attention on the impact of Rik's punch. Look especially at the areas of highlighting on the face, and the hands, reflecting the visual contortions. Ouch! That punch sure did hurt!

If you've successfully completed all the lessons covered in this book, heartiest congratulations! There's still a lot more you can learn if you want to, though. By combining different figures and making them interact with each other, you can start to build up more complex pictures and tell stories.

Overlapping the figures and adding movement lines will take your drawings into a higher realm. And imagine how much more fun you could have by including backgrounds and close-ups, and by drawing lots of different scenes.

Other books in this series deal with these more advanced techniques as well as showing you how to draw robots, animals, and other female characters.

Every drawing you make will bring you another step closer to developing your own personal style. Keep a small sketch-book with you so you can practice drawing all sorts of things you see around you—from people and pets to clothes and cars! You can further improve your skills by working out how some of the characters of well-known manga comics and animes are constructed.

I hope you have discovered the scope for invention and enjoyment that exists in the world of manga, and are now thirsting for that little bit extra.

FABER MOTET SERIES

SERIES EDITOR : GRAHAM DIXON

Masterworks from VENICE

Willaert · Andrea Gabrieli
Merulo · Croce · Finetti
Monteverdi

EDITED BY JEROME ROCHE

FABER ff MUSIC

Masterworks from Venice

CONTENTS

First published in 1994 by Faber Music Ltd
3 Queen Square London WC1N 3AU
Cover design by S & M Tucker
Music processed by Silverfen
German translations by Dorothee Göbel
Printed in England by Halstan and Co Ltd

ISBN 0 571 51286 0